The
Steel String Guitar: Construction & Repair

The Steel String Guitar: Construction & Repair

David Russell Young

Introduction by Jim Crockett,
Publisher/Editor, *Guitar Player Magazine*

CHILTON BOOK COMPANY
Radnor, Pennsylvania

Copyright © 1975 by David Russell Young
First Edition   All Rights Reserved
Published in Radnor, Pa., by Chilton Book Company and simultaneously
in Don Mills, Ontario, Canada, by Thomas Nelson & Sons, Ltd.

Photographs by Bret Lopez, Los Angeles, Ca.
Designed by Cypher Associates, Inc.
Manufactured in the United States of America

Library of Congress Cataloging in Publication Data

Young, David Russell.
  The steel string guitar.

  (Chilton's creative crafts series)
  Bibliography: p.
  Includes index.
  1. Guitar—Construction.   2. Guitar—Repairing.
I. Title.
ML1016.G8Y7   787'.61'2   75-5559
ISBN 0-8019-5959-4

Foreword

This book is directed to anyone interested in steel string acoustic guitars, whether they intend to build an instrument or not. It is a survey of the problems involved in constructing, maintaining, and repairing guitars. Careful attention to the information and instructions which follow will help the guitarist maintain his instrument, guide the novice luthier past pitfalls on the way to building a superior instrument, and prove useful to the amateur and professional repairman.

Guitar technology is in a period of fairly rapid expansion. A number of luthiers are making significant innovations: Roy Noble and Mark Whitebook are worthy of mention in this regard, having improved the structural integrity of the instrument while carrying on the aesthetic tradition of the classic guitar.

The author hopes that this book will be a valuable addition to the technology and a useful tool for those interested in the instrument.

Preface

HISTORY

The origin of plucked string instruments is lost far back in antiquity, and many instruments of this type have come and gone in the last few thousand years in which we have direct evidence of their existence.

The immediate precursor of the guitar as we know it is the Arabic *oud*, brought to Spain by the Moors in the 14th century. In the hands of the Spaniards, a small, ten string guitar called the *vihuela* evolved and, in turn, gave birth to the modern classic guitar. Various types of guitars were used in Europe during the next few centuries, some of which were strung with steel strings. One of these was the *cittern*, which enjoyed considerable popularity before the advent of keyboard stringed instruments.

The steel string guitar used today seems to have been developed by the Austrians in the 18th century. It was brought to America where it became popular as a folk instrument.

An American variation of the steel string guitar, with a large, deep body, was developed in the 1800s and was popularized by the Martin Company as the *Dreadnaught*. The name stuck and can now be considered the generic name for this type of guitar. Many companies produced these guitars in the United States, but only the Martin Company is still in existence. Washburn was another of the important guitar manufacturers during the late 1800s and early 1900s. Today the *Dreadnaught* has become the standard instrument for bluegrass, country and western, and acoustic pop music.

EVALUATING A GUITAR

Whether building or buying a guitar, it is important to be able to judge the quality and condition of an instrument. The most common problem is that the guitar may be difficult to play because of a warped neck, loose frets, or improperly adjusted nut or saddle. The playability of a guitar is referred to as the *action* (see Glossary), and it can be checked by the following procedure.

P-1 European guitar, circa 1800 (*Courtesy of McCabe's Guitar Shop, Santa Monica, California*)

P-2   Martin guitar, circa 1860 (*Courtesy of McCabe's Guitar Shop, Santa Monica, California*)

To check the neck for warping, sight along the edge of the fingerboard, looking down from the peghead toward the bridge. The edge of the fingerboard should appear straight or have a very slight concave bend toward the strings. If there is a concave bend of more than $1/16$ inch (1.6 mm), or if there is any convex bend at all, the instrument will be difficult or impossible to play. Sighting along the edge of the fingerboard will also reveal any loose frets; the ends will appear raised above the ends of the frets that are firmly in place. If you suspect a fret is loose, press the end down against the fingerboard with your thumbnail. If you are right, you will be able to see the end of the fret move slightly.

If the neck is reasonably straight and the frets are all tight, the next step is to check the distance between the strings and the fingerboard. The strings should be within $1/16$ inch (1.6 mm) from the 1st fret and within $1/8$ inch (3.2 mm) of the 12th fret. If the strings are higher than this, the guitar will be hard to play. If the action is too high at the saddle end, it will tend to sound too sharp when played high on the fingerboard because the strings will be stretched excessively in being pressed down to the frets. If the strings are too high at the nut, it will be difficult or even painful to press the strings down to the first fret.

If the string height is reasonable, check the bridge placement by playing the octave on each string (12th fret) and checking the pitch against the octave harmonic at the same fret. The pitch should be the same. (Harmonics are played by touching the string very lightly exactly over the 12th fret and plucking the string.) It is normal for the fretted octave pitch of the second string to be very slightly higher than the harmonic.

If the fretted pitch is higher than the harmonic on all the strings, the saddle is located too close to the nut, and the saddle (or the entire bridge) should be moved toward the nut to shorten the string length. If the discrepancy in pitch is slight, it may be possible to correct it by reworking the saddle (see Chapter 4).

Next, play every note on the fingerboard. Each one should sound clean and clear. If there are local buzzes or rattles, it may be due to worn frets (check for grooves in the frets under the strings), or the nut or saddle may need to be raised slightly. Other possibilities are a loose interior brace; or in the case of guitars with adjustable truss rods, a broken or loose rod. To test for a loose brace, rap the top and back of the guitar with the side of your thumb. If a rattle rather than a clear booming sound is heard, there is probably a loose brace (see Chapter 5). If a high metallic rattle is heard when the neck or peghead is rapped, this may be a loose washer on the tuners, or (perish forbid) a broken truss rod (see Chapter 5).

Another common problem is the bridge pulling away from the top due to excessive string tension or a poor glue joint. Look along the edge of the

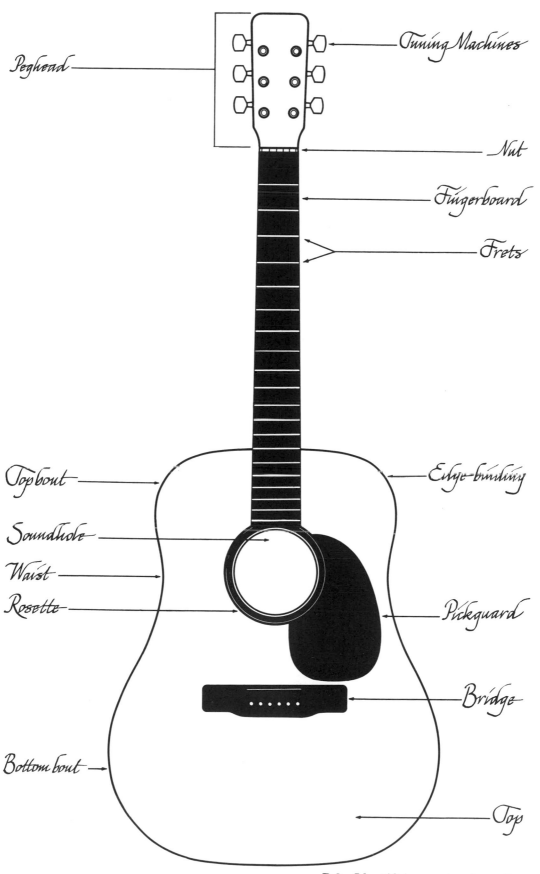

Peghead

Tuning Machines

Nut

Fingerboard

Frets

Top bout

Edge-binding

Soundhole

Waist

Rosette

Pickguard

Bridge

Bottom bout

Top

P-3   Identifying parts of a guitar

bridge where it meets the top, on the opposite side from the strings. If there is any gap, the bridge is being pulled from the top. It should be removed and re-glued after the glue surfaces have been thoroughly cleaned (see Chapter 5 for removing bridge).

Look all over the guitar for cracks, separated joints, or separated edge binding. Check the tuners for wear by noting whether they turn smoothly or have excessive backlash when tuning up and down. If all the above factors check out, the instrument is mechanically sound.

This leaves that great nebulous property generally referred to as "tone." Opinions vary enormously as to what constitutes good tone quality, but the following may serve as a reasonable guide. Loudness is usually a valuable attribute, and it should be fairly uniform throughout the range of the instrument. There is no such thing as "overbalanced trebles"—this just means underbalanced basses. Loudness is particularly valuable in a bluegrass guitar, since the guitar tends to get lost when competing with a banjo. The instrument should also sustain tones long enough to hold the music together when playing slowly.

"Tone quality" boils down to overtone structure, and the author's preference is for a strong fundamental tone with a full overtone structure. Too few overtones make a guitar sound cold and empty, but too many high overtones produce a dissonant and "tinny" sound. This is still largely unexplored territory in guitar design; hopefully much more will be known in the near future.

If you follow the procedure outlined above, you will avoid most of the pitfalls in choosing or evaluating a guitar. Beyond this, let your fingers and ears be your guide—if pickin' it makes you grin, that is the whole point.

CRAFTSMANSHIP

Like most things, craftsmanship is a matter of degree. No one would undertake a job such as building a guitar with an intention to do shoddy work; but in the course of completing such an involved and demanding project, the best of intentions can be slowly worn away—along with the patience of a saint or the skin on one's knuckles. However, with a little foresight, control, and determination, the frustration and disappointment of a seriously flawed piece of work can probably be avoided.

First, don't bite off more than you can chew. If you have little experience in woodworking or a modest assortment of tools, settle for a simple instrument made of easy-to-work materials. The museums can wait until your second or third effort to enshrine your genius. Remember that a simple piece of work, well executed, is far more pleasing than something very complex but imperfectly done.

Second, form a clear picture of each step before you rip into it. Exotic hardwoods can display the capriciousness of a kitten and the resistance to your will of national politics. If you are not wide awake while working, you can expect your results to be lumpy.

When performing any task for the first time, one is particularly likely to make errors. If you blunder horribly through ignorance, have the integrity to throw away what you have ruined. You don't even have to tell anyone. Don't spoil otherwise good work by trying to salvage a piece of pretty but damaged wood: beautiful materials *exaggerate* defects. If you make a mistake, stop and figure out why. If you are tired, stop and come back when you are fresh.

When you finish sanding something, set it aside for a while, then go back and sand out the scratches you missed the first time. Before applying a finish, look over every square inch of surface as carefully as if you were going to marry it. Keep your wits and your tools sharp.

David Russell Young

Contents

List of Black & White Illustrations

List of Color Illustrations

The
Steel String Guitar:
Construction
& Repair

Introduction

Ever since the Egyptian god Hermes stretched some gut string across an old tortoise shell, man has been fascinated with the guitar—not just with its sound, but also with its form. The guitar, and its many predecessors over the centuries, has always had to fulfill a triple function: it had to appeal to the ears of the performer and the audience; it had to please the guitarist's sense of touch and balance; and it had to be visually beautiful.

In an effort to satisfy all three needs, luthiers have created guitars in shapes as varied as circles and triangles; and there have been oval ones, rectangular ones, bowl-shaped and pear-shaped ones; and ones built of animal sculls, of woods of every type, of assorted metals, cooking pots, and cigar boxes. The Ripley collection of oddities even boasts a guitar made from a chamber pot.

But a guitar does not succeed apart from its sound. Much as a wooden dresser is useless if its drawers don't slide, a lovely guitar is worth nothing if its tone is dead and if it doesn't project well. And here lies the fascination with the luthier's art. The craftsman is faced with a two-part challenge: to satisfy both art and science. On the one hand, the instrument must attract the eye; on the other, it has to be playable, dependable, and possess that elusive quality—the right sound.

A good luthier need not be a guitar player. In fact, many of today's best builders can't play the guitars they create. They are able to tune them, to tell if their tone is too strident or too muddled, to tell if the intonation is accurate. If you don't play guitar, don't be discouraged: no one expects a performer to be able to build his guitar, so why should a luthier be expected to play? Each person is an artist in his own right. The act of an instrument's creation can surely be satisfaction enough. Ample are the rewards in building a guitar: designing your own mosaic rosette and fitting it perfectly around the soundhole, setting the thin binding strips around the guitar's edges so wood end grains can't be seen, inlaying the fingerboard precisely with your own carefully cut mother-of-pearl designs. Even the meticulous tying of the strings to the tuning machines can be aesthetically enjoyable.

Certainly music itself can be a most sensuous experience, but no more so than working carefully and patiently with the luthier's materials to slowly carve a gracefully arched top, delicately bend a gently sloping side, or endlessly rub in a satin-smooth luster. So the rewards of playing a guitar and building one are plentiful, but not at all dependent upon each other.

The classical nylon string guitar has a world-wide history that is virtually lost to antiquity. Books exploring its past and detailing with the instrument's construction are readily available in most bookstores and libraries.

The steel string guitar, however, is a different matter. Its foundations lie in the United States as an instrument of folk artists, cowboys, and back-country blues players. The steel string guitar came into its own barely fifty years ago, and so lacks the "legitimate" history of the classical guitar: it doesn't reach back to well-known European craftsmen; it isn't displayed in the world's museums; it's not the focal point of orchestral compositions.

The steel string acoustic guitar is loud, frequently raucous, and delicacy is often lost on it. And while it is essentially a coarse, rough instrument, it is a guitar of the people—it's loud without needing electricity, it rings out above singers, yet is still as portable as its nylon or gut strung predecessor. Thus, it is one of the most popular musical instruments in the world.

There is a paradox here, however: while the steel string guitar is so much in demand, the literature on it is almost non-existent. Craftsmen who want to build them, musicians who want to maintain them, and service managers who want to repair them are in a bind. Books on building and repairing classical guitars are of little or no help, because the steel string is a unique instrument. Granted, there are certain obvious similarities between the two types of acoustic guitars, but the differences are numerous and of great importance. For instance, the tension caused by the steel strings is enormous and can cause guitar necks to twist or bow, can pull a bridge right off the face of a guitar, can make an instrument's top buckle or split, and can pull the tuning keys loose, causing the guitar's pitch to slip. So the builder of a steel string guitar finds himself or herself faced with such peculiar problems as embedding metal truss rods in the instrument's neck, shaping unusual interior wooden struts that will keep the guitar's body from bursting at the seems, and affixing bridges that are strong enough to hold the strings in place without totally killing the vibrations of the guitar's top.

Mr. Young's book combines two distinct, yet related, things: a basic, readable introduction to the craft and a rare step-by-step guide to building that first guitar. The author's objective, though, isn't to teach the beginning craftsman how to immediately create the world's greatest guitar. His goals are more long-range than that. He warns, "Don't bite off more than you can chew . . . The museums can wait for your second or third effort to enshrine your genius. Remember that a simple piece of work, well executed, is far more pleasing than something very complex but imperfectly done."

Young wants to see people use his book as a framework for later, experienced development. With that aim in mind, he sets out to show you how to construct this one, specific steel string guitar. And rather than inundate you with massive numbers of subtle alternatives to every problem a luthier has to confront, he leads the way toward a single, proven method—a method which he formulated during the construction of his own hundred-plus guitars. The result is that you may, by precisely and carefully following the author's steps, build your own guitar with a minimum of wasted effort, time, material, and money.

Bret Lopez' superior photographs go hand-in-hand with the text to detail minute stages of construction, as well as provide the needed overviews of the building process. Together, Young and Lopez guide you through such general areas as wood selection and tool use into specifics of bracing the top and back, building the rosette, fitting the truss rod, leveling the frets, finishing the wood, shaping the neck, carving the bridge, and much more.

The end product of all this diligent work, however, is something that neither Young's crisp writing nor Lopez' graphic photos can fully explain. It comes when the new luthier holds that initial guitar as gently as a mother cradling her first baby—a pride in long and hard work, but work done well. After that initial rush, though, the pride can tend to obscure something that can bring even greater joy—a careful, clinical evaluation of the craftsmanship involved.

The objective eye looks at the beading of the edge binding and notices how even it is; inspects the guitar's inside and notes the cleanliness of the many glued joints; observes the smoothness and consistency of the highly polished finish; studies the rosette, your *own* rosette, and finds how even the mosaic is and how perfectly it fits into place; scans the instrument's back to see how well the two matched panels meet neatly at the center seam; views the care with which the tuning keys were installed. Then, a first cautious, almost hesitant tuning, an initial delicate strum followed by a more robust and assured one, and you know you've done it—you've made a first guitar that really isn't bad, not bad at all. And you can't wait to begin work on Number Two.

David Russell Young has succeeded.

Jim Crockett
Publisher/Editor
Guitar Player Magazine

1   Tools & Materials

WOOD

When choosing wood, care must be taken to pick well-seasoned, dry materials. Even carefully made guitars may crack when subjected to sudden or severe climatic change, but it is important to minimize this possibility. Unseasoned wood will feel unusually heavy due to a high water content and will be more difficult to cut, with a tendency to clog or gum up saw teeth.

Sight along each piece of wood to check for warping, and examine all surfaces for checks. Examine the end grain carefully for hairline cracks. Caution in selecting materials can save time, money, and temper during construction. Imperfect materials preclude the possibility of perfect work.

TEMPERATURE, HUMIDITY, AND SEASONING

One generally thinks of wood as a stable, solid, homogeneous material; but when cut into thin sheets and exposed to variations in temperature and humidity, it is found to change dimensions in surprising and sometimes alarming ways.

Wood consists of patterns of cells of varied sizes and densities, woven through with capillary-like passages which carry sap in the growing tree. Moisture is constantly being absorbed from and released into the atmosphere as the wood reacts to heat and humidity changes. A vivid example of what this can mean to the novice luthier is the case of a guitar back which is braced at 60% relative humidity and is later found to have reversed its arch when the humidity drops to 20%, so that the back is concave rather than convex in shape. The same hydraulic power that operates when a growing tree buckles a concrete sidewalk is constantly at work in any piece of wood. Although the scale is smaller, the forces can still be quite strong. It is important to have an understanding of these factors in order to build durable instruments.

This process is complicated by the fact that the moisture exchange

 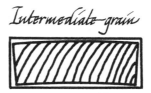 

1-1   Wood distortion during seasoning. Outside lines indicate cross-section dimensions of green wood; inner lines indicate dimensions of seasoned wood.

process occurs much more rapidly in the end grain, where the ends of the natural moisture passageways are exposed, than in other wood surfaces. The combinations of grain pattern and moisture loss distortion are shown in Figure 1-1.

The first consideration when choosing wood is seasoning. Green lumber has a very high moisture content which drops gradually over a period of years as the wood simultaneously shrinks. Eventually the moisture content of the wood depends on the moisture in the surrounding atmosphere. This process is often accelerated by placing lumber in a large kiln and exposing it to high temperatures to drive off the excess moisture, thereby stabilizing the wood. Whether kiln dried or air dried, it is important that wood be seasoned before use. Otherwise the shrinkage that occurs will produce cracks, warpage, and separated joints.

The seasoning process operates from outside toward the inside of a piece of wood. Thus it must operate more rapidly on thin pieces of wood, such as that in the guitar body, which have a high surface-to-volume ratio. It is therefore advisable to age guitar wood for some time in the rough, 3/16 inch thick stage to allow uniform seasoning. After joining and thinning, the wood ideally should be allowed to stand again for several months before assembly.

During assembly, it is important to brace and assemble the body in a low-humidity atmosphere to minimize the possibility of cracking. A constant 20 percent humidity would be nearly ideal. You will need some kind of instrument to measure relative humidity. Inexpensive hygrometers are usually very inaccurate; a wet and dry bulb thermometer is better, and a sling psychrometer is the best (and the most expensive) instrument for measuring relative humidity.

Once assembled, the body becomes quite strong and resistant to humidity deformation; but it is important to have the wood at its smallest dimension during construction so that it will not be placed in tension when the humidity drops due to the moisture loss shrinkage. You need not worry about strains on the guitar caused by taking it from the low humidity atmosphere. The wood will absorb some moisture, but the absorbent end grain is sealed by the edge binding. Whatever expansion of the wood does occur is not important; it is rapid drying that produces cracks.

High heat can be a very damaging force on guitar. Hot, direct sunlight can blister the finish, and the cooking effect of the heat can drive the moisture out of the wood, causing it to crack. Never leave a guitar in its case in the sunlight, as this acts as an oven, producing temperatures as high as 150°F. A closed, dark colored car also acts as an oven in hot weather.

BUYING WOOD FOR YOUR GUITAR

Unfortunately the size and thicknesses of woods sold for guitar materials is not standardized. Thicknesses may vary within the same piece, and pieces are often irregular in shape.

If you are buying materials by mail order be sure to state the minimum sizes for the components, or you may receive pieces too small for a steel string guitar. (Be especially careful with tops, backs, and sides which are often cut for the smaller classic guitar.)

If you are able to select your woods personally, take along a half-pattern of the top and your side template. Materials often contain defects which can be avoided by laying out the patterns so that the defects fall in a waste area. If your pattern is at hand, you will know at once if a particular piece of wood is useable.

You may have to buy a large piece of wood and re-saw it for some components such as bracing. If this is the case, allow for losses in cutting for vertical grain and possible hidden defects in the wood. Sap pockets, tiny cracks and checks, and worm holes are often not noticeable until the pieces have been cut to size.

Here is a list of suggested materials for your first guitar. These are the most readily available and easiest to work of the optional woods.

> Back, sides, and neck: Honduras mahogany
> Top: Redwood or cedar
> Edge binding: Maple
> Bridge, fingerboard, and peghead overlay: Rosewood

OPTIONAL GUITAR WOODS

Back and Sides

The woods most often used for backs and sides are Honduras mahogany, East Indian rosewood, and Brazilian rosewood. *Honduras mahogany* is the least expensive of the three, and the easiest to work with. It is easy to obtain, easy to bend, easy to cut and sand, and easy to finish. Also, it is less likely to crack than either type of rosewood. The beginner is well advised to use mahogany for his first guitar. Be sure not to confuse Honduras mahogany with Luan or Philippine mahogany, which is not suitable for guitars.

East Indian rosewood is a hard, heavy, straight-grained wood, ranging in color from brown to almost purple. Under finish, the color darkens and a deep luster appears. This wood is more expensive and more difficult to work than mahogany, but it gives a fuller tone and richer appearance to the instrument.

Brazilian rosewood produces the richest grain effects and is the most spectacular under finish. However, it is less stable than East Indian rosewood, harder and more dense, therefore more difficult to work and more likely to crack. It is scarce and expensive and more likely to contain defects. While it is almost universally preferred for fine classic guitars, luthiers sometimes prefer the tonal quality of East Indian rosewood for steel string guitars.

Maple and walnut are also suitable for backs and sides and may produce an instrument with excellent tone. Both woods are widely available and less expensive than rosewood, and both have the added advantage of being fairly easy to work. Maple has the further advantage of being easier to finish, as it is a closed-grain wood and does not require filling.

Top

Tops may be made of European spruce, Sitka spruce, Coast redwood, or American red cedar. *European spruce* has traditionally been used on the finest instruments; it is straight-grained, even colored, light, and strong. It is in short supply and expensive. Alternatively, *Sitka spruce* is cheaper and more readily available. It tends to have a less straight grain and more color variation than European spruce.

Cedar has only recently been introduced as guitar top wood. It is cheaper than comparable quality spruce, more available, and less likely to crack because of its greater stability. While top quality European spruce tops are very hard to obtain, excellent quality cedar is fairly easy to find. Cedar has been finding favor among the best classic guitarmakers in Spain and elsewhere. *Redwood* is similar to cedar in stability, but softer. The color of redwood is an attractive reddish brown under lacquer.

Fingerboard

It is customary to use *Gaboon ebony* for the fingerboard of top grade guitars. *Brazilian rosewood* is the second choice. If rosewood is chosen, Brazilian is favored over East Indian because it is harder and has a more attractive grain. Ebony has the advantage of being harder and more resistant to wear from strings and fingernails; and it is preferable to rosewood if mother-of-pearl inlays are to be used, since the black provides better contrast for the light inlay. Unfortunately ebony is rare, expensive, difficult to work due to brittleness, and prone to cracking.

Bridge and Neck

Bridges are usually made of *rosewood or ebony*, chosen to match the fingerboard.

Piece	Quantity Needed	Dimensions	Type of Woods Usable
Top	(2)	8″ x 20″ x ³⁄₁₆″ (20.3cm x 51cm x .5cm)	Spruce, cedar, or redwood
Back	(2)	8″ x 20″ x ³⁄₁₆″ (20.3cm x 51cm x .5cm)	Honduras mahogany, rosewood, or maple
Sides	(2)	4¹⁄₂″ x 32″ x ³⁄₁₆″ (11.5cm x 81.3cm x .5cm)	Honduras mahogany, rosewood, or maple (same as back)
Neck	(1)	3″ x ¹¹⁄₁₆″ x 28″ (7.6cm x 1.7cm x 71cm)	Honduras mahogany
Fingerboard	(1)	2³⁄₄″ x ³⁄₈″ x 18″ (7cm x .95cm x 45.7cm)	Ebony or rosewood
Linings	(4)	¹⁄₂″ x ³⁄₁₆″ x 30″ (1.3cm x .5cm x 76.2cm)	Basswood
Peghead Overlay (6-string)	(1)	6¹⁄₂″ x 3″ x ¹⁄₁₀″ (16.5cm x 7.6cm x .25cm)	Ebony or rosewood
Peghead Overlay (12-string)	(1)	8″ x 3″ x ¹⁄₁₀″ (20.3cm x 7.6cm x .25cm)	Ebony or rosewood
Top Block	(1)	1¹⁄₂″ x 3″ x 3³⁄₄″ (3.8cm x 7.6cm x 9.5cm)	Honduras mahogany
Bottom Block	(1)	¹⁄₂″ x 2¹⁄₂″ x 4³⁄₄″ (1.3cm x 6.4cm x 12.1cm)	Honduras mahogany
Edge Binding	(4)	31″ x ¹⁄₄″ x ¹⁄₁₀″ (78.7cm x .64cm x .25cm)	Rosewood or maple
Bridge (6-string)	(1)	7″ x 1¹⁄₄″ x ³⁄₈″ (17.8cm x 3.2cm x .95cm)	Ebony or rosewood
Bridge (12-string)	(1)	7″ x 1¹³⁄₁₆″ x ³⁄₈″ (17.8cm x 4.6cm x .95cm)	Ebony or rosewood
Back Bracing	(4)	³⁄₈″ x ¹⁄₂″ x 16″ (.95cm x 1.3cm x 40.6cm)	Honduras mahogany
Top Bracing, 6-string	(1; A)	³⁄₈″ x ³⁄₄″ x 11¹⁄₂″ (.95cm x 1.9cm x 29cm)	Honduras mahogany
	(2; B & C)	³⁄₈″ x ¹⁄₂″ x 18″ (.95cm x 1.3cm x 45.7cm)	Spruce
	(1; E)	³⁄₈″ x ¹⁄₂″ x 10¹⁄₄″ (.95cm x 1.3cm x 26cm)	Spruce
	(1; F)	³⁄₈″ x ¹⁄₂″ x 9″ (.95cm x 1.3cm x 22.9cm)	Spruce
	(2; G & I)	¹⁄₄″ x ¹⁄₂″ x 5″ (.6cm x 1.3cm x 12.7cm)	Spruce

Piece	Quantity Needed	Dimensions	Type of Woods Usable
	(2; H & J)	¼″ x ½″ x 4″ (.6cm x 1.3cm x 10.2cm)	Spruce
	(1; L)	¼″ x ¼″ x 3″ (.6cm x .6cm x 7.6cm)	Spruce
	(2; K & M)	¼″ x ¼″ x 3¾″ (.6cm x .6cm x 9.5cm)	Spruce
	(1; D)	1/10″ x 2″ x 5½″ (.25cm x 5.1cm x 14cm)	Spruce
Top Bracing, 12-string	(1; A)	⅜″ x ¾″ x 11½″ (.95cm x 1.9cm x 29cm)	Honduras mahogany
	(2; B & C)	⅜″ x ½″ x 18″ (.95cm x 1.3cm x 45.7cm)	Spruce
	(1; E)	⅜″ x ½″ x 10¼″ (.95cm x 1.3cm x 26cm)	Spruce
	(1; F)	⅜″ x ½″ x 13″ (.95cm x 1.3cm x 33cm)	Spruce
	(1; G)	¼″ x ½″ x 13¾″ (.6cm x 1.3cm x 34.9cm)	Spruce
	(4; H, H′, J, & J′)	¼″ x ¼″ x 3¾″ (.6cm x .6cm x 9.5cm)	Spruce
	(1; I)	¼″ x ¼″ x 3″ (.6cm x .6cm x 7.6cm)	Spruce
	(1; D)	1/10″ x 2″ x 5½″ (.25cm x 5.1cm x 14cm)	Spruce
Purfling	(2)	31″ long (78.7cm long)	
Fretwire		50″ (127cm)	
Nut and Saddle		(1 each, standard sizes)	Ivory or bone
Tuning Machines		(1 set)	

Necks are almost always made of *Honduras mahogany;* it is very stable, strong, and easy to shape. *Rosewood or maple* are occasionally used for necks if a more interesting grain effect is desired.

Edge Binding and Blocks

The edge binding may be made of *wood or plastic.* Plastic is easier to use than wood, but some plastics have a tendency to shrink over a number of years and come loose from the guitar. Wood must be pre-bent to shape and is more difficult to fit since it is much stiffer than plastic.

Rosewood can be used for edge binding if a dark color is desired, or maple may be chosen for a lighter color.

The top and bottom blocks inside the guitar should be *Honduras mahogany;* this gives a reliable glue joint and solid support. Do not use basswood.

Linings and Bracings

Basswood is good for linings because it is easy to bend, very stable, and easy to glue. *Mahogany or well-seasoned pine molding strips* (available at lumberyards) may be substituted.

Top bracing should be dry, straight, vertical grained *spruce.* Back bracing and the brace under the end of the fingerboard should be *Honduras mahogany* cut from vertical grain stock.

DIMENSIONS OF WOOD NEEDED

The list on pages 8 and 9 gives precise dimensions for cutting pieces; the quantity needed of each piece; types of woods which may be used; and for the bracing pieces, corresponding labels for placement as shown in Figures 2-42 and 2-43a.

TOOLS

Many fine guitars have been made using only a few basic hand tools. Minimum tools are a coping saw, back saw, plane, scraper, chisel, knife, file, drill, hammer, combination square, and straight edge. These tools can be used to make most other specialized tools or jigs. Some other useful tools are shown in Figures 1-2 and 1-3.

POWER TOOLS

If available, power tools can save a great deal of time. An electric drill and a router of Dremel Moto-Tool® are among the most useful. A drill press, orbital sander, belt sander, and circular saw can likewise prevent a great deal of unnecessary drudgery.

HAND TOOLS

A special tool, a purfling groove cutter, is required for cutting the edge binding recess if a router is not available. Since the purfling groove cutter shown in Figure 1-2.j is rather expensive, you may prefer to make the tool shown in Figure 1-4.

It can be made of any hard wood. The cutter is a no. 2 X-Acto® knife with a no. 23X blade. Eight 1½-inch machine screws are needed, with a

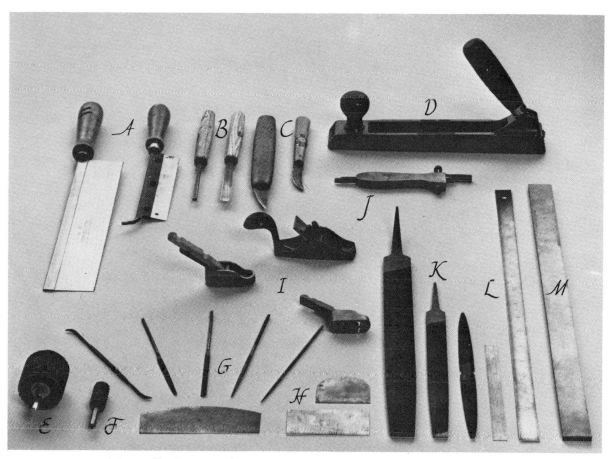

1-2 a. Fret saw and razor saw
    b. ¼″ straight and ½″ curved gouges
    c. Knives
    d. Stanley® Surform
    e. Sanding drum
    f. Rotary rasp
    g. Needle files
    h. Curved violin-maker's scrapers and straight cabinet scraper
    i. Miniature block plane and finger planes
    j. Violin-maker's purfling groove cutter
    k. Files: 12″ single cut with tang bent up for levelling frets; 8″ mill bastard
       for trimming fret ends; and double-pointed half round rasp
    l. 6″ and 18″ machinist's scales
    m. ¼″ x 1″ x 18″ dimension-ground steel bar for straight edge

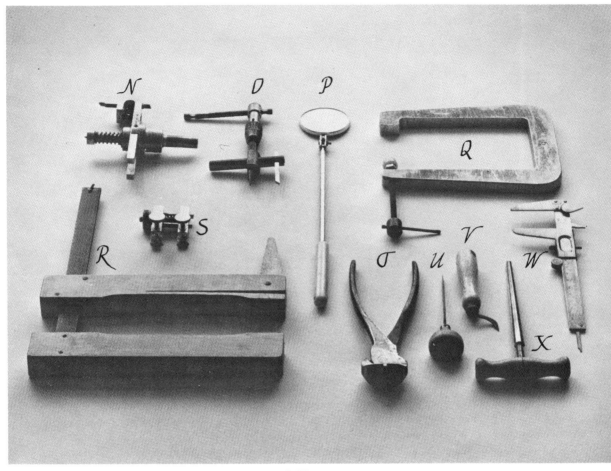

1-3 n. Commercial circle cutter for use in a drill press
   o. Circle cutter with plumb bob tip for center point and handle with chuck
      attached for hand use
   p. Inspection mirror
   q. Bridge clamp, bandsawed from ½″ aluminum
   r. Deep throat cam clamp
   s. Violin-maker's crack clamp
   t. End cutters (Channellock®)
   u. Engraving tool (for engraving details on inlays)
   v. Violin purfling groove cleaner—a very narrow chisel for tight quarters
   w. Violin peghole reamer
   x. Calipers

1-4 Cutter for edge binding groove

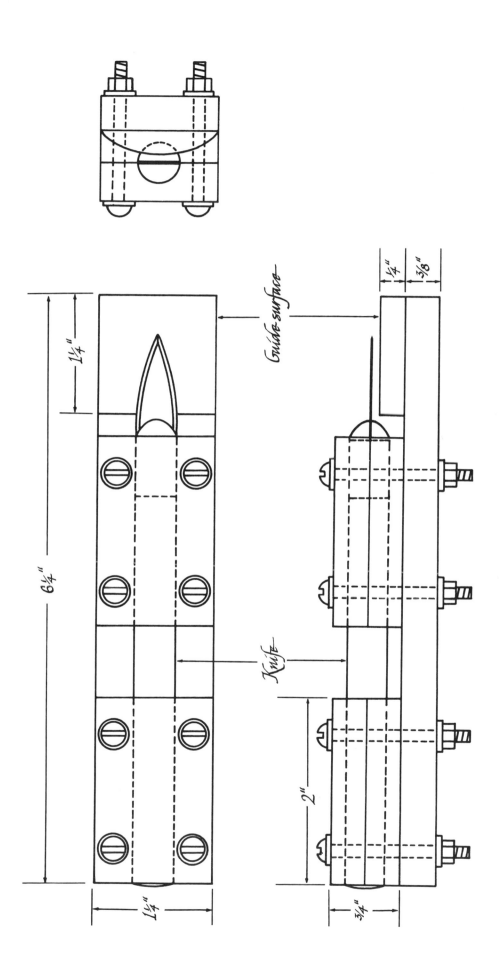

Guide surface

Knife

$6\frac{1}{4}''$

$1\frac{1}{4}''$

$1\frac{1}{4}''$

$\frac{1}{4}''$

$\frac{3}{8}''$

$2''$

$\frac{3}{4}''$

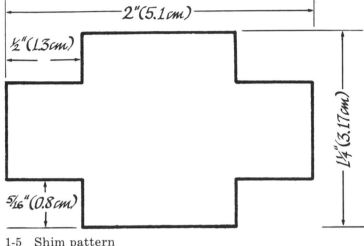

1-5   Shim pattern

hex nut and two washers for each. Cut two ¾" x 1¼" x 2" blocks and drill a ⁷⁄₁₆-inch diameter hole down the center of each to make the blocks which hold the knife handle. Cut a 1¼" x ⅜" x 6¼" piece and epoxy a 1¼" x 1¼" x ¼" piece to the end for the curved guide surface; shape the guide as shown in the end view drawing. Clamp the two blocks which were drilled to hold the knife to the block with the curved guide as shown in the drawing, and drill holes for the eight screws. The holes are centered ³⁄₁₆ inch from the side and ⅜ inch from the ends of the blocks. Cut the blocks which will hold the knife down the middle as indicated in the drawing.

The tool can now be assembled. The screws must be tight enough to keep the knife from twisting when in use, so it is a good idea to make the blocks such that the grain runs perpendicular to the axis of the knife handle. This will lessen the risk of cracking the wood when tightening the screws. The width of cut can be adjusted by inserting shims made of paper, cardboard, or any other convenient material between the knife holding blocks and the long block with the guide surface on the end (Figure 1-5). A tool which does not have a provision for adjusting the width of cut is useless unless one uses square bindings of only one size.

CLAMPS

A number of clamps, wooden or metal, are needed for assembly. Eight 4-inch C-clamps or sliding bar clamps are necessary for holding sides in the mold after bending and while gluing on the top, and three deep-throat clamps are essential for gluing on the bridge. It is hardly possible to have too many clamps and having too few will be a constant annoyance.

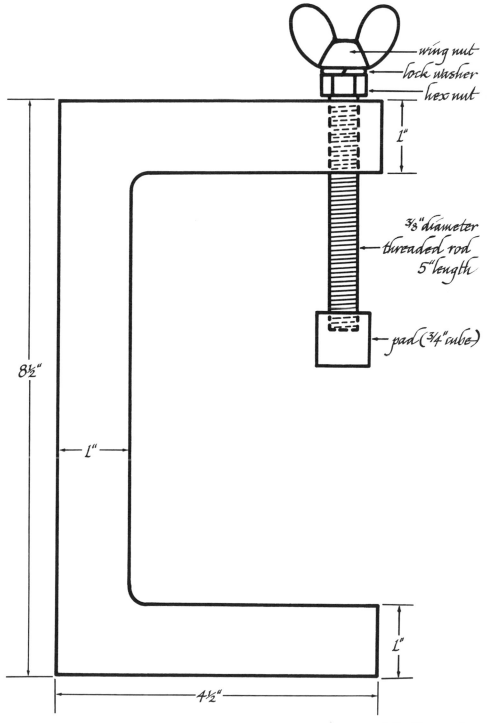

wing nut
lock washer
hex nut

1"

3/8" diameter
threaded rod
5" length

pad (3/4" cube)

8½"

1"

1"

4½"

1-6 Clamp plan

At least twenty 6½-inch clamps are needed for gluing on the top and back. The clamps shown in Figure 1-6, can be made for a fraction of the cost of cast iron clamps. They are cut from ¾-inch plywood, and the screws are 5-inch lengths of ⅜-inch diameter threaded rod (available at hardware stores). The "handle" is a wing nut held in place with a hex nut and lock washer. Drill a hole with a size "P" drill (0.323 inch), and bevel both ends of the hole with a countersink. The threaded rod can be twisted into the hole with finger pressure, and it will cut its own threads in the wood. This arrangement will not stand heavy pressure or prolonged use, but little pressure should be used when clamping on tops or backs, so these clamps should serve for building many instruments. The pad on the end of the screw is a ¾″ x ¾″ block of ¾-inch plywood, drilled ¼ inch with the size "P" drill.

Should it become necessary, the female threads can be renewed by drilling out the hole and epoxying in a piece of heavy-wall tubing with the appropriate inside diameter. Threads can then be tapped into the metal tube, and the clamps can be used indefinitely.

SHARPENING TOOLS

It is important to keep edge tools sharp, and this in turn requires the proper tools: a Carborundum® stone, an Arkansas stone, and light oil. New edge tools should be sharpened before use (X-Acto blades included) and frequently thereafter.

GLUE

There is a school of thought which holds that only animal hide glue is acceptable for musical instruments. This is probably true for instruments of the violin family, which are designed for easy disassembly and which are quite strong structurally. A guitar, however, is relatively fragile and more highly stressed. Furthermore, steel string guitars often see rather hard use. Airline travel is particularly hard on guitars. Other hazards are belt buckles, microphones, and musicians of uncertain equilibrium who fall down stairs and off stages. There is one guitarist who has been known to chew entirely through the top of a guitar with finger picks during a single number, in a great outpouring of adrenalin and spruce splinters. Other guitar catastrophes known to the author include being trod upon both by people and horses, as well as being run over by cars.

In view of the hazardous existence which guitars are exposed to, it seems wise to give the instrument every possible structural advantage, including the best possible glue joints. Hide glue has some disadvantages in this respect. It absorbs water from the atmosphere and joints can fail if exposed to stimultaneous stress and dampness. It has also been demon-

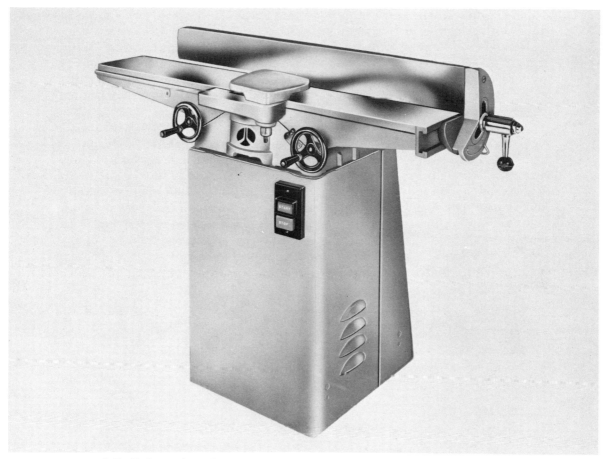

1-7 Deluxe long-bed jointer (*Courtesy of Rockwell International, Power Tool Division*)

strated that fungus spores can live in animal glue and eventually break down the glue bond. Since the guitar is not designed for easy disassembly, the relative ease of separating hide glue joints is not a relevant point for guitar construction.

In lieu of hide glue, plastic resin glue is well suited for many phases of guitar construction. Titebond®, made by Franklin Glue Company, is a yellow aliphatic resin glue which sets quickly, is very strong, and allows cleaning off excess with a damp cloth. It is superior to white or polyvinyl glues for guitarmaking purposes. Titebond is commonly available in hobby shops. If you can't obtain it locally, write to the manufacturer for the local distributor in your area. Since Titebond contains water, it should not be used for any of the joints in the neck, since the wood will absorb some of the moisture and tend to warp.

Glue joints which are highly stressed or cover large areas should be done with epoxy, which gives maximum strength. AMR 101-m® is an excellent epoxy, very strong, and resistant to high temperatures. Clamp time is about 24 hours, with maximum strength being reached in about a week. Epoxy should be used for all joints in the neck, the rosette, and for attaching the neck to the body. AMR is available through Erika Banjos, 14731 Lull, Van Nuys, CA 91406.

It is very important to make any surfaces which are to be glued mate as accurately as possible. The optimum thickness of the glue line is on the order of one-half to *one-thousandth* of an inch. These are very close tolerances for a machinist, let alone a woodworker; but it is important to try for the best glue joints, since this is the point at which guitars usually come apart. Glue surfaces should be clean and smooth. There is no advantage to roughening the surface; this results in a poorer glue bond. Rosewood should be wiped with lacquer thinner or mineral spirits to remove excess oil. It also helps to use as many clamps as possible so that pressure will be evenly distributed and all excess glue will be squeezed out of the joint.

2 The Guitar Body

BUILDING THE MOLD

The mold is one of the most important jigs (see Glossary) used in building the guitar and should be constructed very carefully to avoid problems during assembly of the guitar. A mold is necessary for bending the sides and for holding the sides in position while assembling the body of the guitar.

It is important that the mold be as dimensionally stable as possible; therefore, it should be made of plywood or composition board. It is false economy to cobble up a mold out of bits and pieces of lumber. Such a mold will almost certainly warp due to unbalanced stresses as the wood ages. Even if the mold is made of seasoned lumber, it may very easily warp out of shape. A block of seasoned wood has come into dimensional equilibrium in a particular shape; and if that shape is changed (as in sawing out the shape of a guitar body), new surfaces are exposed and shrinkage occurs due to exposure to the air.

Whether plywood or composition board is used, construction procedures are the same. Cut ten 30″ x 10″ pieces from ³/₄-inch thick stock and laminate them into two stacks, each 3³/₄ inches thick. To ensure good glue joints, at least ten clamps should be used on each stack. Glue the layers together two at a time using Titebond.

If you try to glue up an entire half of the mold at once, the glue may begin to set before the joint is clamped tight, the pieces will tend to slip out of alignment, and the excess glue will make a troublesome mess. When making a glue joint, always use just *slightly* more glue than necessary. When clamped tight, a small amount of glue should be squeezed out all along the edge of the joint.

When both halves of the mold blank are laminated, the edges which correspond to the centerline must be jointed so that they are perfectly straight and square. This is tedious work to do by hand with plane and scraper. Try to get the job done on a power jointer by a cabinetmaker or at a lumberyard that does millwork. If the joint is properly finished, the two halves of the mold will mate perfectly when laid on a flat surface and pressed together.

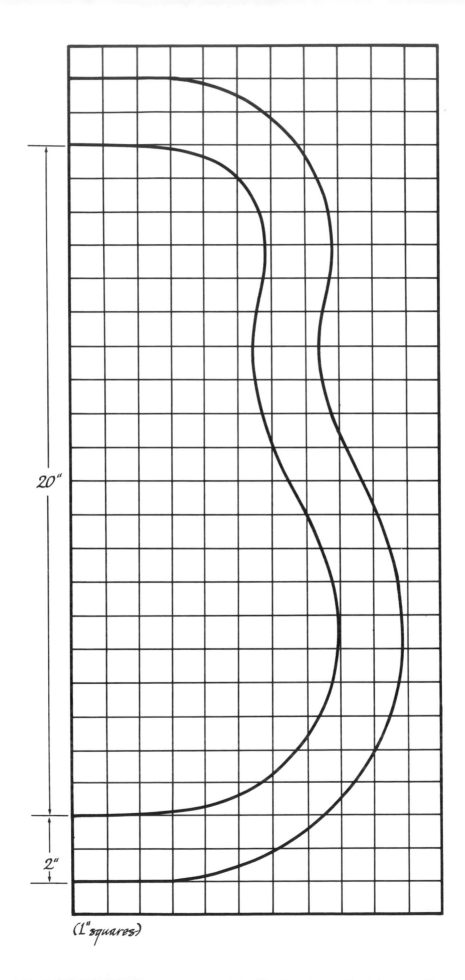

20″

2″

(1″ squares)

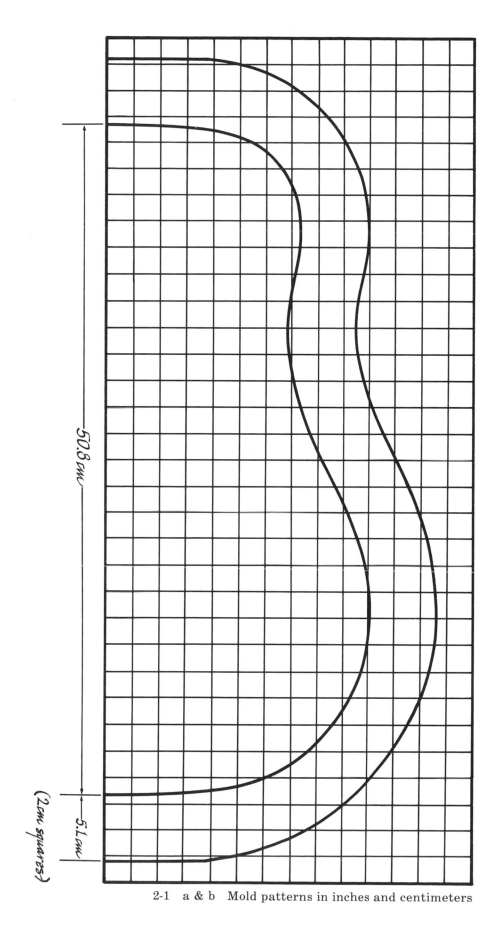

50.8 cm

5.1 cm

(2 cm squares)

2-1   a & b   Mold patterns in inches and centimeters

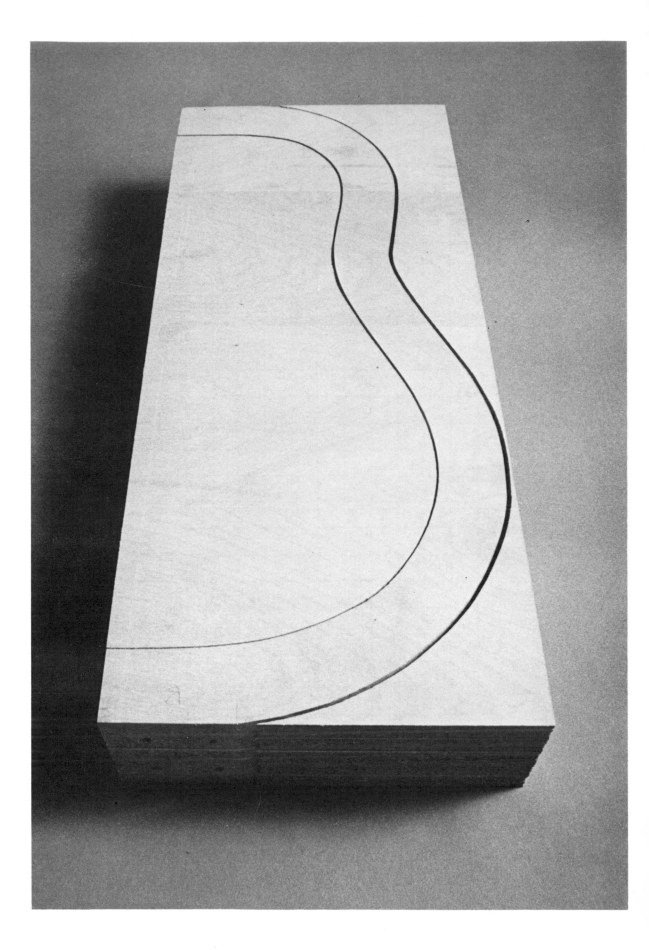

Enlarge the pattern shown in Figure 2-1 and transfer it to a sheet of heavy pattern paper or illustration board. Cut out a template for the mold, being very careful to cut the inside contour accurately. Lay this template on the mold blanks and scribe the outline of the mold with a knife point. Don't use a pencil to mark the outline — a scribed line is much easier to follow accurately with a saw.

Bandsaw the outer waste portion away first so that the mold blank will be easier to handle when cutting the critical inside contour. Use a ¼ inch blade, and check the angle between the saw blade and work table with a try square. The blade must be exactly perpendicular to the wood. Cut out the inside of the mold, working just up to the scribe line. You will then have pieces corresponding to those in Figure 2-2.

CUTTING THE END PLATES

Using the plan shown in Figure 2-3, cut out two end plates and assemble the mold, using 2-inch wood screws. The end plates can be made of

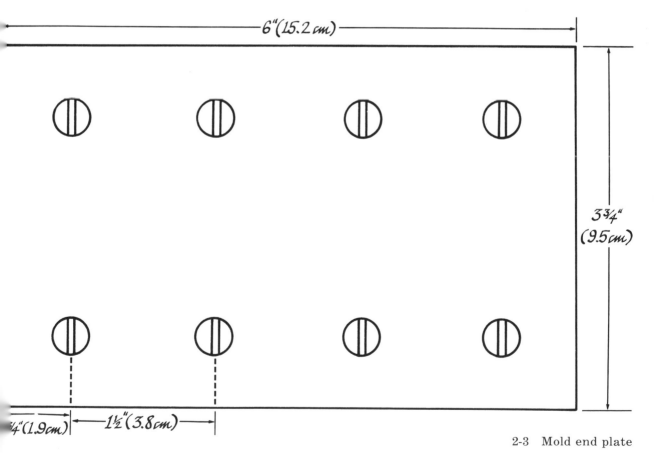

2-3   Mold end plate

2   Mold blank after bandsawing

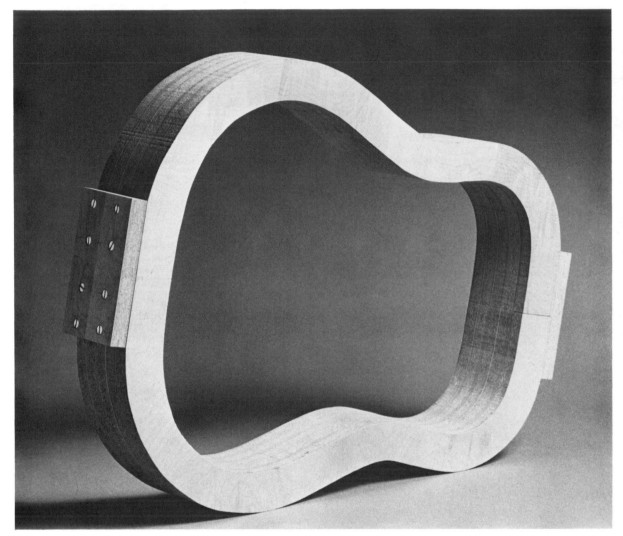

2-4 Assembled mold

¾-inch plywood or ¾-inch particle board. Waste left over from the mold blank will also work. Be sure to work on a flat table or on the floor when drilling holes and assembling the pieces. The finished mold must lie perfectly flat and have perpendicular walls. The finished mold is shown in Figure 2-4.

JOINING THE TOP AND BACK

The primary problem in splicing the halves of the top and back is to get a perfect joint between the halves. (Whether you start with the top or the

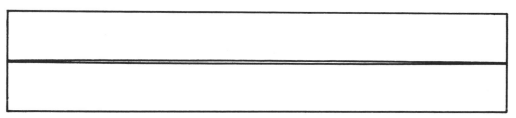

2-5 Spring joint

back, the procedure is the same.) If you have access to a properly set up jointer, this can be done in a matter of minutes. If the job is to be done by hand, it can be an exasperating experience.

The center joint should be accurate to within a few thousandths of an inch. A gap of 1/64 inch is too much; it will leave a pronounced line where the glue is not squeezed out when the joint is clamped, and the likelihood of the joint coming apart is far greater than if the job had been properly done. To check the accuracy of the joint, lay the two halves down on a flat surface, press them together so that the pieces are aligned; then carefully lift them up, squeezing the pieces together to keep them in alignment. Hold them up to a light and very carefully examine the joint to see if any light passes through. One can see discrepancies of just a few thousandths of an inch this way.

If the two ends of the joint meet perfectly and there is a very slight gap (about 0.005 inch or 0.13 mm) in the center which can be made to disappear when the two pieces are firmly pressed together, a perfect glue joint will result. This is called a *spring joint* (see Fig. 2-5) and it pre-stresses the wood against the strain produced by a humidity drop, thus lessening the chances of cracks due to humidity changes.

If the two halves meet perfectly all along the joint, the glue joint will be perfect; but the likelihood of cracks produced by humidity fluctuation will be slightly higher than if a spring joint were used. Such fine distinctions are not as important for a comparatively stable wood (such as Honduras mahogany or Canadian cedar) as they are for a difficult wood (such as Brazilian rosewood). Either joint is acceptable; but in the case of rosewood, it is preferable to try for a spring joint.

If the joint meets in the center but has gaps at the ends, do it over. This type of joint is apt to come apart or lead to cracks.

The grain of the two halves of the back or top should be bookmatched as nearly as possible. That is, the grain pattern of one side should be the mirror image of the grain on the other side.

USING A JOINTER

If you are using a jointer, follow this sequence of operations. First, determine which sides match most closely. Unless the grain is perfectly vertical, material may have to be planed from one side to produce a perfect match. Run the edges over the jointer until straight, then examine the surface of the joint very carefully for *checks* (see Glossary). If you do find a check in the edge, cut away more wood until it disappears. Checks are rare, but they can be very troublesome if they are not discovered at this time.

Lay the pieces flat, press the jointed edges together, and see if the grain matches. If necessary, trim one side until it does. Now fold up the two halves as if they were the pages of a book and run them slowly over the jointer, making a very light cut. Check the accuracy of the joint. A perfect fit can be made into a spring joint by pressing the wood down lightly at the beginning of the cut, bearing down in the middle, and easing up at the end.

If it seems impossible to get a good joint, the jointer may be improperly set up. To work perfectly, the beds must be parallel and the cutter head must be exactly level with the out-feed table.

Jointing by Hand

If you are jointing the pieces by hand, the procedure is basically the same. First, plane the edges approximately straight and trim until the grain matches. Final fitting of the joint may be done with a file.

Sandpaper can be glued with rubber cement to a flat, rigid surface (such as a drawing board) and used to true the edge. A strip of wood should be clamped across the sandpaper and used as a fence, holding the piece you are working with against it and sliding the edge back and forth

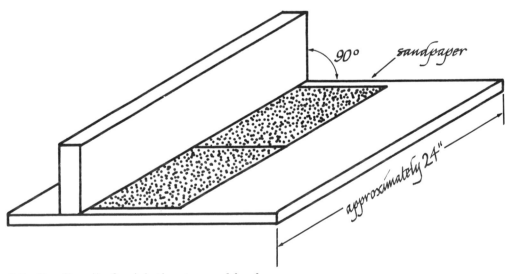

2-6 Sanding jig for jointing top and back

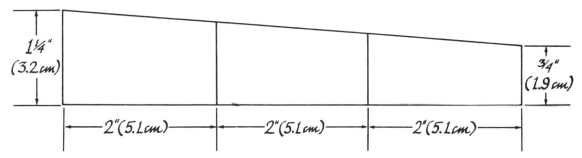

2-7 Clamping wedges

on the sandpaper. Make sure the fence is perpendicular to the sandpaper surface (see Fig. 2-6).

To glue the halves of the top and back together, you need a piece of ¾ inch plywood at least 18″ x 24″ (45 cm x 60 cm), and three straight pieces of any kind of wood 1″ × 2″ × 24″ (2.5 cm × 5.1 cm × 60 cm). Cut three wedges of any hard wood according to the plan in Figure 2-7. Any piece of scrap wood could be used for wedges, but the author has found through experience that it is easiest to do it this way. The wedges are big enough to tap in place conveniently with a hammer and no time is wasted hunting around for a piece of scrap just the right size for the middle wedge.

Clamp or screw one of the strips to the edge of the plywood board. (Refer to Figure 2-7 as you work.) Lay the two pieces to be glued on the board with a strip of waxed paper underneath the joint. Line up the wedges so that they apply pressure uniformly on the center and on each end of the piece to be glued, and clamp a strip of wood against the opposite side as in Figure 2-8. (A strip of contrasting veneer can be glued in the center of the back.)

Now coat the joint with glue and align the edges. Clamp a strip of wood over the joint so it won't pop up when pressure is applied, using a second piece of waxed paper to keep the clamping strip from sticking to the glue joint (see Fig. 2-9). Tap the wedges snug and let it dry overnight.

When removing the clamps, knock out the wedges first so the clamping pressure won't buckle the glued piece and break the joint.

THINNING THE TOP, BACK, AND SIDES

Before cutting out shapes for the top, back, and sides, the entire rough piece must be thinned. This prevents thinning the material too much at the edges, which inevitably occurs if the parts are cut out before thinning.

The traditional method for thinning wood for the body of the guitar is by hand, with plane and scraper. The simplest way is to find a cabinet

2-8   Back ready to clamp

2-9   Center clamped down and pressure applied

shop or mill with a large drum sander which has an endless belt feed system. Such a machine can sand the wood to close tolerances in very little time, at a reasonable cost. A hand type belt sander can also be used, but great care must be taken to keep the thickness of the wood even. Besides economy of effort, sanding has an advantage over the plane in that it does not tend to dig in, tear, or chip when figured wood is used.

If you are using a plane, clamp the wood to the top of the workbench and make light cuts, using a very sharp plane held at a 45° angle to the direction of cut to reduce the chance of tearing the wood. Check the thickness often and be careful to keep it uniform. Final thinning and removal of marks can be done with a scraper.

The *back* and *sides* should be between 0.09 inch and 0.10 inch (2.3 mm to 2.5 mm) thick. Thicker wood is hard to bend, and thinner wood is too fragile. The *top* should be between 0.10 inch and 0.12 inch (2.5 mm to 3 mm) thick, depending on the stiffness of the individual piece of wood.

Flex the wood across the grain to judge stiffness. A stiff top will tend to sound a clear, ringing tone when held by a corner and tapped sharply with the knuckles. Such a top can be worked thinner than one which is less stiff and duller in tone. Very flexible tops, sometimes hardly stiffer than cardboard, should not be used.

CUTTING AND BENDING THE SIDES

Transfer the side template plan (Fig. 2-10) to a piece of heavy pattern paper. Lay the wood for the sides end to end, finish side up, with the ends that are to be at the bottom joint butted together. Check to see that the grain pattern matches. If necessary, trim until the grain matches as closely as possible. With a plane or jointer, straighten the edges that will join to the top. Tape the sides together so that the grain matches and scribe the outline of the template onto the sides (Fig. 2-11). Carefully cut the sides to shape with a coping saw or bandsaw, then sand the edges.

Now you will need a 12-inch piece of 2½-inch or 3-inch diameter aluminum pipe with a ⅛-inch wall thickness. Make a baffle for the end out of a tin can lid as shown in Figure 2-12; this will prevent too rapid heat loss. The bending iron is clamped in a vise and heated with a propane torch as in Figure 2-13. To test the heat of the iron, wet your fingertip and tap it against the iron; it should be hot enough to make a sputtering sound.

Wet a piece of the excess wood trimmed from the sides and try to bend it by placing it against the iron and applying gently pressure while moving the wood constantly. Don't rest the wood in one place and wait for it to bend—this produces a series of bumps in the sides. Check constantly to keep the bend an even, fair curve. If the wood is scorching, lower the heat. Be sure to keep the wood damp and work slowly and carefully, checking the bend against the mold as work progresses. When you get the feel of it, you are ready to bend the sides.

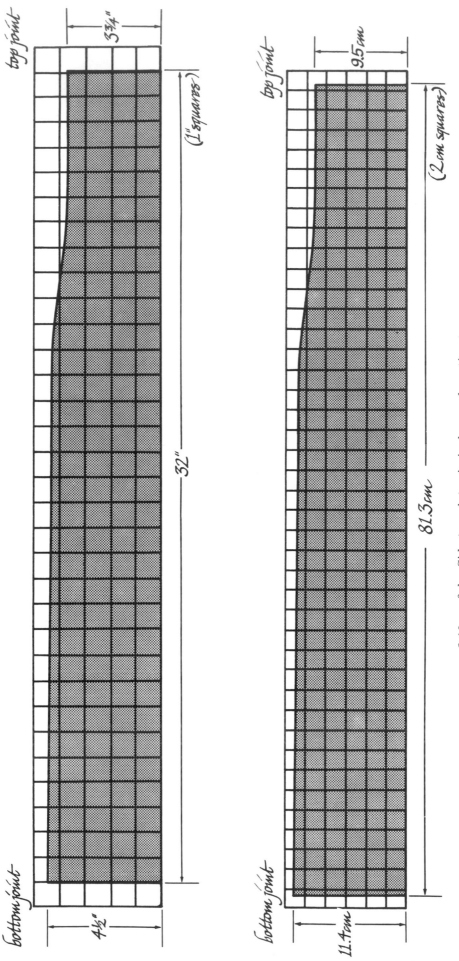

top joint

3¾"

(1 squares)

32"

4½"

bottom joint

top joint

9.5 cm

(2 cm squares)

81.3 cm

11.4 cm

bottom joint

2-10 a & b Side templates in inches and centimeters

2-11 Scribing outline of sides

2-12 Bending iron and baffle

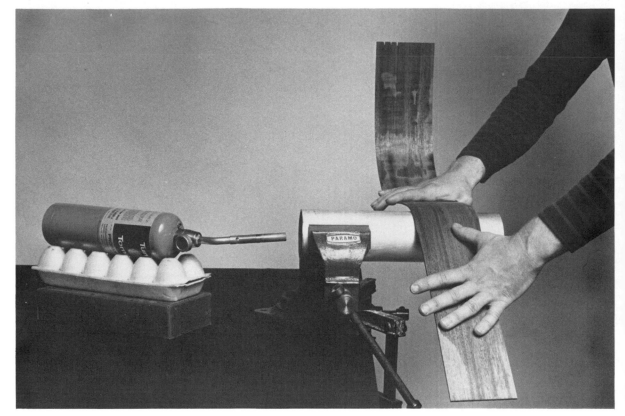

2-13   Bending the sides

Rosewood should be soaked overnight before bending. The bathtub is fine for this—but weight the sides so that they remain completely submerged. Water temperature is unimportant, since it will turn to steam when it hits the bending iron. The oil in the rosewood will seep out and blacken from the heat; but this will sand off.

Mahogany sides can be soaked under a tap just prior to bending. Keep water and a sponge handy while working so that the wood does not get too dry and scorch. If you bend the wood too much in one spot, turn it over and correct the bend.

When the sides are bent so that they conform to the mold, clamp them into the mold as in Figure 2-14. Start in the middle and clamp the ends last. Leave the sides in clamps overnight. Almost all of the moisture will have been driven out of the wood during the bending process; there is no need to leave the sides clamped up for days. Before removing the clamps, use a knife (or any sharp point such as a needle or awl) to scribe the sides along the ends of the mold so that the ends can be trimmed to a perfect joint.

2-14   Sides bent and clamped in the mold

PREPARING THE SIDES FOR THE TOP AND BACK

After the newly bent sides have set overnight in the mold, remove them, and sand the inside surface to remove residue left from bending. Trim the ends along the lines scribed while the sides were still in the mold and make any necessary adjustments so that the ends butt perfectly. After trimming and sanding, the sides are returned to the mold and waxed paper is inserted between the sides and the mold to prevent the sides from being glued to the mold.

The top and bottom joints are reinforced by Honduras mahogany blocks. Do not use any other wood for this purpose. These blocks (one of each shape as given in Figs. 2-15 and 2-16) may be of one piece or laminated, but if solid blocks are used, the grain must run perpendicular to that of the sides. If laminated blocks are chosen, make the grain of the end laminations run parallel to the grain of the sides. This makes fitting

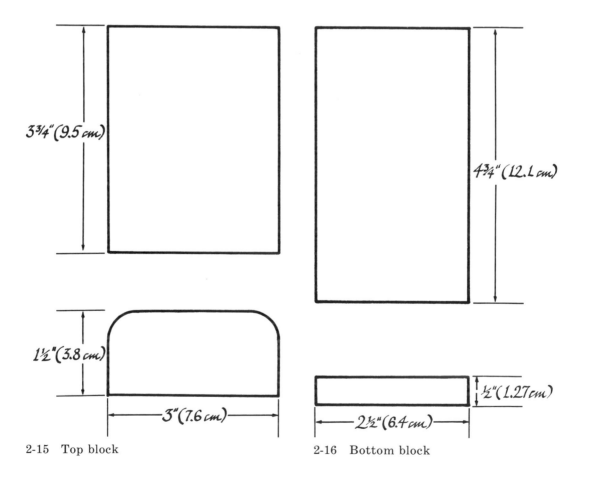

3¾" (9.5 cm)

4¾" (12.1 cm)

1½" (3.8 cm)

½" (1.27 cm)

3" (7.6 cm)

2½" (6.4 cm)

2-15 Top block

2-16 Bottom block

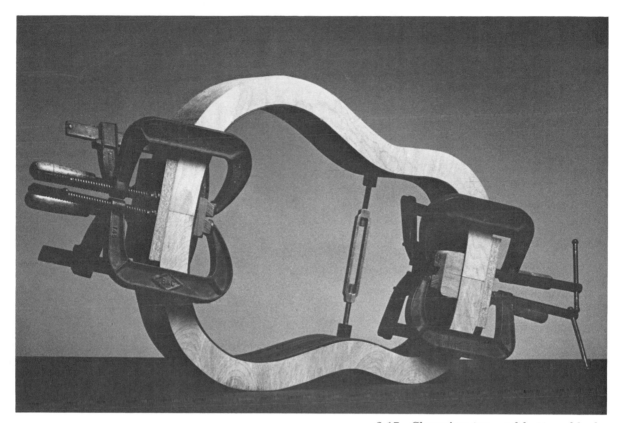

2-17 Clamping top and bottom blocks

the top and back easier, since it will not be necessary to plane across end grain.

These blocks must be very carefully fitted to the contour of the sides because they are very critical to the structural integrity of the instrument. As a convenience, the author uses a standard turnbuckle with the eyes cut off the screws and wooden pads substituted. A piece of scrap wood trimmed to the appropriate length may also be used here to hold the waist.

See Figure 2-17 for clamping arrangements. Note that the sides project out of the mold at the bottom, requiring additional clamping with small clamps as in Figure 2-18.

In order to conform to the top which will later be braced and arched, the sides must be contoured to match the curvature of the top before gluing in the top linings. Figure 2-19 shows the proper curvature for the top; about ⅛ inch should be removed from the sides at the top and bottom blocks, with gradually less wood cut away as the waist is approached. (The apex of the curve is at the waist.) Take care to keep the curvature fair

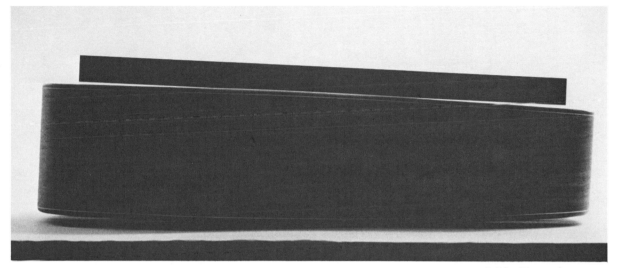

2-19   Top curvature

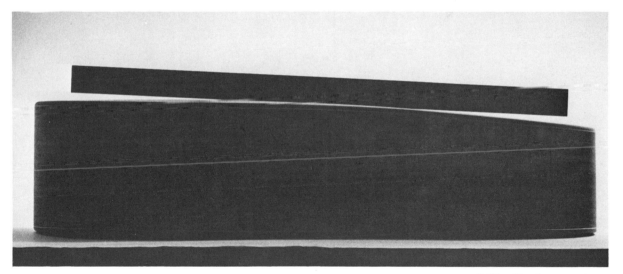

2-20   Back curvature

and smooth. The curvature of the back is shown in Figure 2-20 for comparison.

LININGS

Linings must be fitted to provide a gluing surface for the top and back. The easiest and probably the best method is to use basswood strips sawn nearly through at ⅜-inch intervals, as in Figure 2-21. It is important

2-18   Clamping protruding part of bottom block

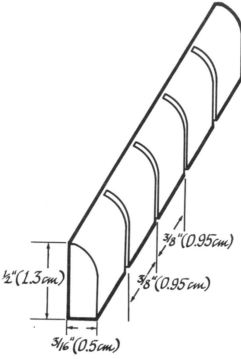

2-21   Linings

that the inner face have a flat surface parallel to the gluing surface for clamping purposes—linings that are triangular in cross section are difficult to clamp in place.

Clothespins make very satisfactory clamps for linings provided one uses heavy-duty wooden clothespins and wraps them tightly with size 64 rubber bands to increase the clamping strength. Crowd the clothespins on as close as they will go. Don't worry if the linings break—just line up the broken ends as you glue them in with Titebond (Fig. 2-22). As soon as clamping is finished, scrape away excess glue.

In order to minimize the possibility of cracked sides, it is wise to glue reinforcing bars across the sides as in Figure 2-23. Spruce, mahogany, or rosewood are all very satisfactory for this purpose. See Figure 2-24 for reinforcement dimensions and Figure 2-25 for placement diagram. Cloth tape is sometimes glued to the sides for reinforcement, but this is only a halfway measure which provides very little strength.

It is traditional to inlay a wedge of rosewood or ebony over the bottom joint of the sides. Use material the same thickness as the sides, making sure the outside edges are straight. Cut the wedge about 1 inch longer than the width of the sides at this point to allow for fitting (see Figs. 2-26 and 2-27).

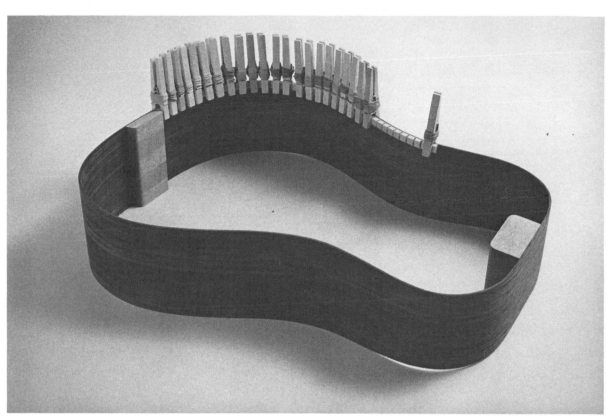

2-22 Gluing in linings

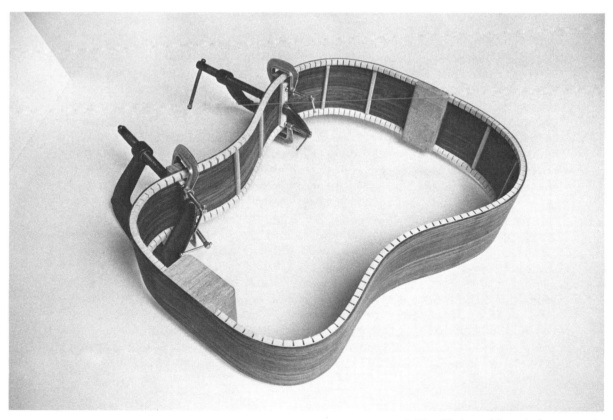

2-23 Gluing side reinforcements

2-24   Side reinforcements

Clamp the wedge in place and scribe the outline with a sharp knife or single-edge razor blade. Clamp the end block in a vise and carefully cut along these scribe lines with a razor saw, then remove the wood between the lines with a ¼ inch straight chisel. Glue in the bottom wedge, beveling the edges if necessary to obtain a snug fit. Glue with Titebond and leave in clamps overnight. Figure 2-28 shows the sides ready for fitting the top and back.

MAKING A ROSETTE

It is traditional to inlay a decorative ring around the soundhole of the guitar. This practice began with the carved soundholes of the Arabic oud and its descendent, the lute. The Spanish vihuela retained the traditional carved decoration; but when the guitar evolved from the vihuela, the soundhole was left open in order to produce greater volume and the decoration was moved to the top. Furthermore, the rosette is not just an ornament: it reinforces a weak point in the top and helps prevent cracks which might develop from the end grain exposed by the soundhole.

The simplest rosette is made of strips of wood veneer, either dyed or natural color. Black should be used for the outer margins. This defines the rosette visually and conceals any slight gaps that might be present around the edge. Dyed veneers are available commercially, or leather dyes (available in shoe repair shops) can be used to dye holly veneer. Holly should be used for light colored strips. Maple is easier to get, but it is much less attractive under finish.

The rosette is traditionally the hallmark of the individual luthier; therefore, the reader is encouraged to develop his own design. Try to keep the width of the rosette close to ⅜ inch and make the design symmetrical.

Construction of the rosette is fairly simple. A circle the same size as the inside diameter of the rosette is cut from a sheet of ⅛-inch plywood. Cover the edge of this circle with plastic tape to prevent excess glue from

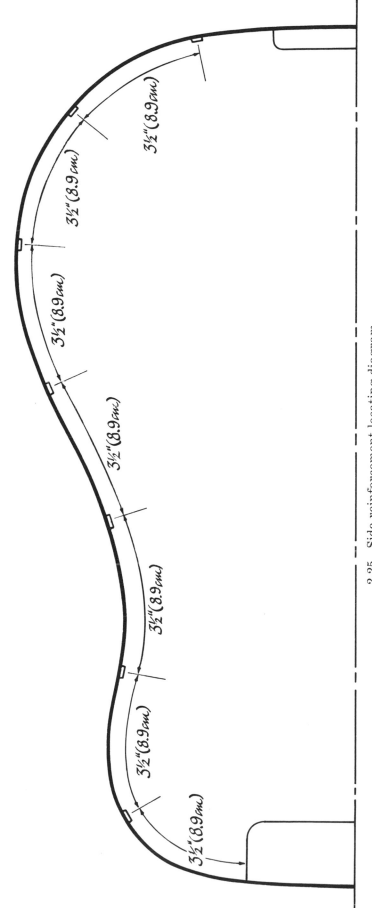

2-25 Side reinforcement locating diagram

3½"(8.9 cm.)

3½"(8.9 cm.)

3½"(8.9 cm.)

3½"(8.9 cm.)

3½"(8.9 cm.)

3½"(8.9 cm.)

3½"(8.9 cm.)

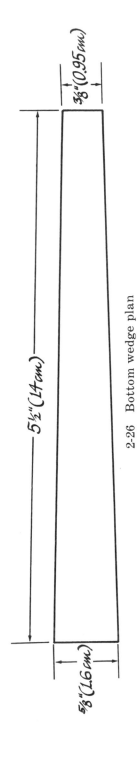

2-26 Bottom wedge plan

2-27 Fitting bottom wedge

sticking to it (refer to Fig. 2-29). Cover a piece of soft scrap wood (basswood or redwood are best) with waxed paper and fasten the plywood disk to this backup board with three screws.

If you are making a simple veneer rosette, coat the veneer strips with epoxy and hold them in place with push pins as in Figure 2-29. A strip of veneer should be coated with soap or beeswax and wrapped around the outside of the rosette proper to prevent the pins from damaging the outer ring. Leave the rosette in a warm place until the epoxy sets hard; then remove the rosette from the form and sand or scrape both sides clean and smooth. The finished rosette should be about 1/16 inch thick (1.6 mm).

An abalone rosette is more complex and requires a special sanding drum and an electric drill or drill press to turn it. Two veneer rings are needed, one to go inside the abalone and one for the outside. A disk with a diameter equal to the outside diameter of the ring of abalone must be made for a gluing form to make the outer veneer ring.

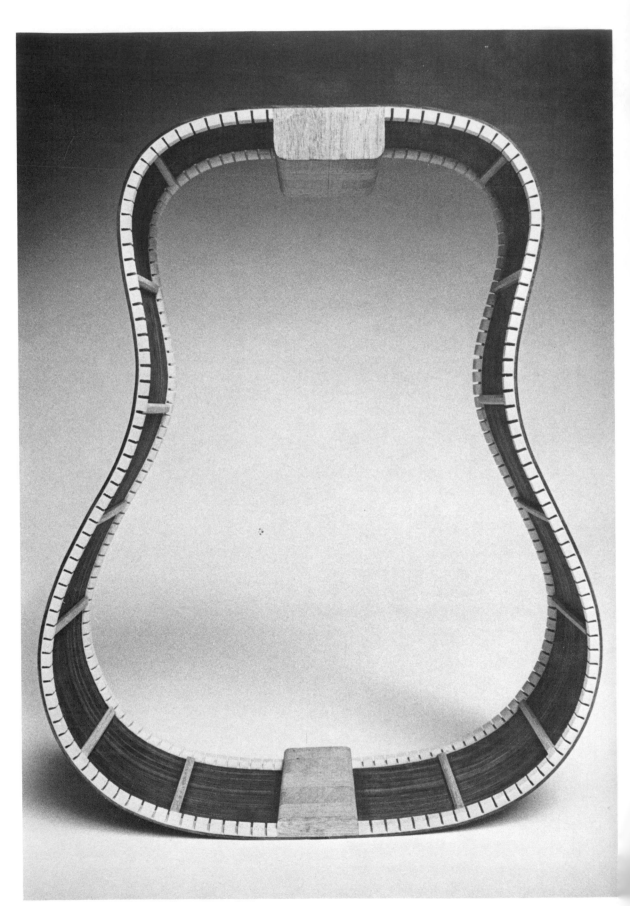

2-28 Sides, ready for top and back

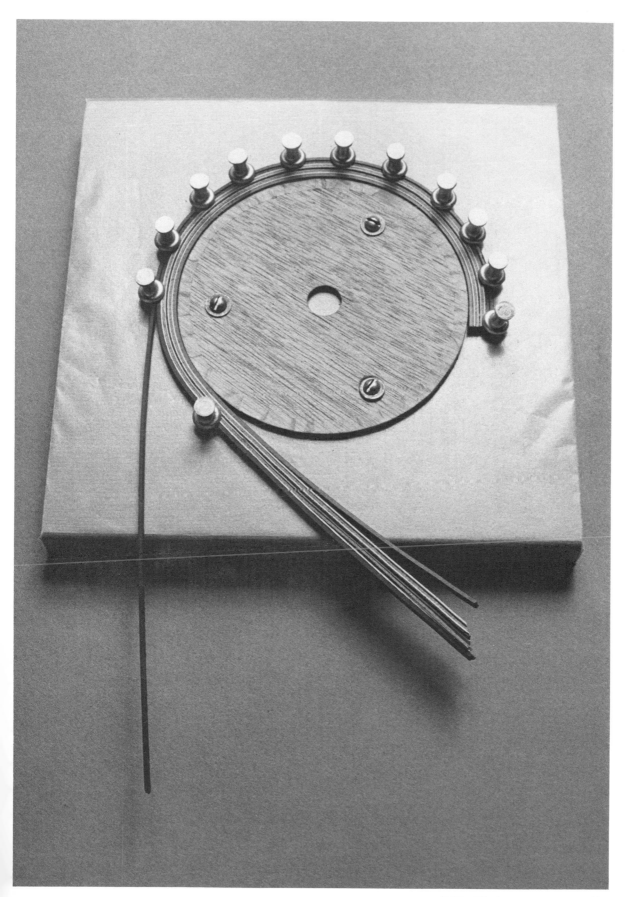

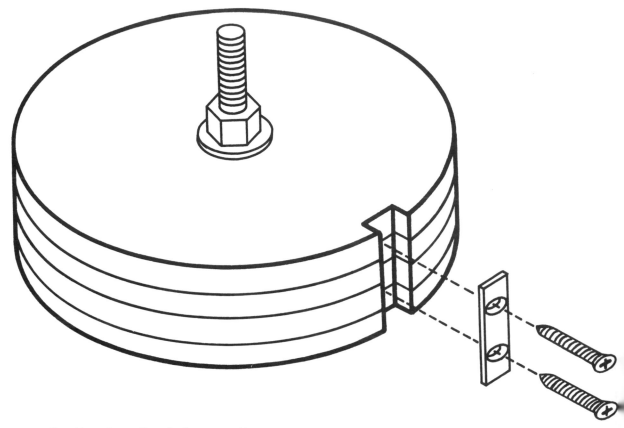

2-30   Sanding drum for abalone rosette

Black and white (holly) or colored veneers may be used, but each ring should have a black veneer strip on both inner and outer margins to visually minimize glue lines.

To cut the segments for the abalone ring, a special sanding drum is necessary (see Fig. 2-30). To make the drum, cut four disks of ¼-inch plywood. The diameter should be the diameter of the inner ring gluing disk plus twice the width of the inner ring.

Drill a ¼-inch hole *precisely* in the center of each disk. Coat the disks with Titebond, thread them onto a 2 inch long by ¼ inch diameter machine screw, and tighten the nut down to squeeze the disks together. Use washers on both sides of the plywood "sandwich." Place small clamps (six or eight one-inch clamps) around the perimeter of the disks to squeeze them tightly together all around; then clean away all excess glue with a damp rag. Set in a warm place overnight to dry.

Next, chuck the end of the screw into a drill press or electric drill and turn it on. If the center holes were accurately drilled, the drum should run nearly true. Cean up the outside edge by holding a sanding block with #120 sandpaper against the drum while it is rotating.

Now cut a recess for the batten (made from a piece of scrap sheet aluminum or brass) (Fig. 2-30). Drill two screw holes in the batten, and two holes in the bottom of the recess.

Cut a one inch wide strip of #80 emery cloth from a sanding belt (size 3″ x 18″ is cheap) and wrap it around the side of the drum. Tuck the ends under the batten, making sure that the screws go through both ends of the emery cloth, then tighten the screws to hold the cloth snugly around the drum.

Using this tool in an electric drill or drill press, grind the inner radius into abalone blanks as shown in Figure 2-31; you should use thick blanks ("2 ligne," about 0.05 inch thick). One ounce of abalone blanks is enough material for a rosette; blanks are available from Erika Banjos (see List of Supplies).

2-31   Grinding inner radius of abalone segments

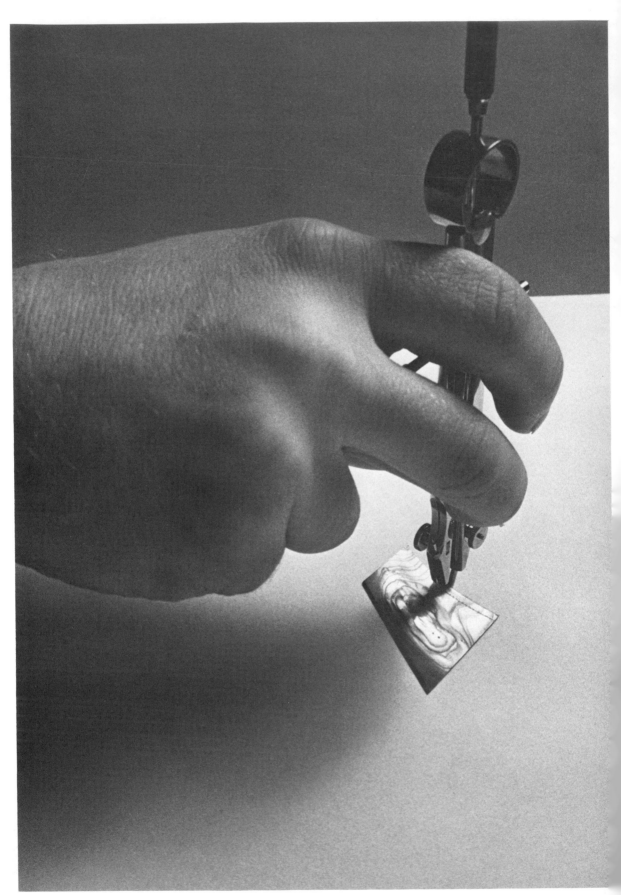

2-32 Marking outside contour of abalone segments

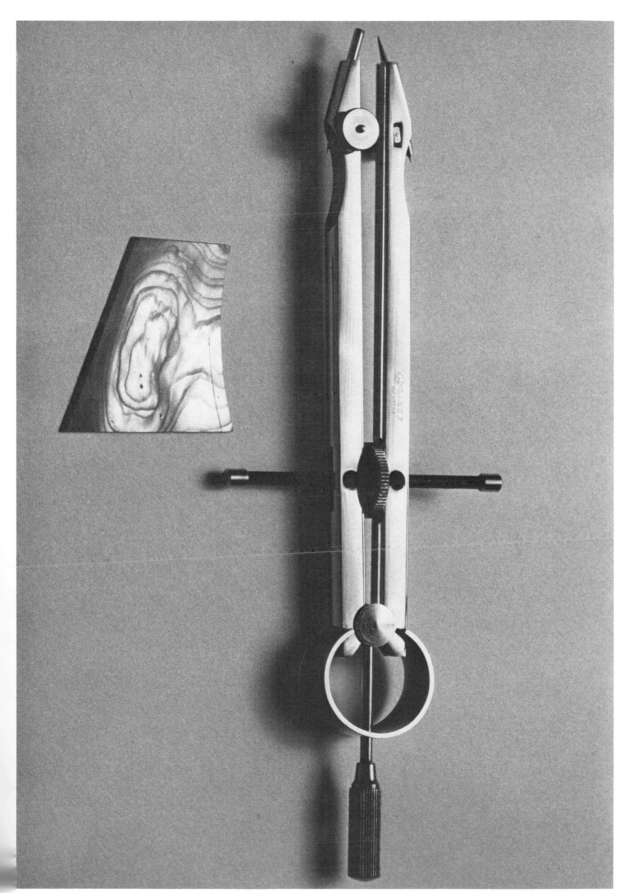

2-33　Compass and scribed abalone blank

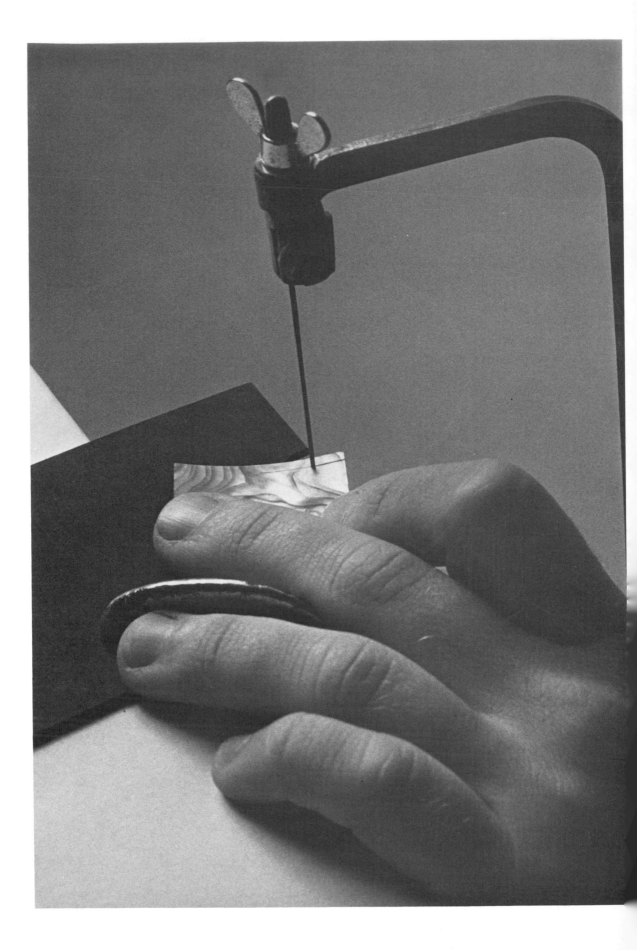

Next the outside radius must be cut. A simple way to do this is to scratch the outside contour onto the blank as shown in Figure 2-32. Using an ordinary draftsman's compass or dividers, turn one of the points around so the blunt end can be used as a guide (see Fig. 2-33). Segments should be about 0.1 inch (2.5 mm) wide. Taking care not to go off the scribed line, cut out the pieces using a jeweler's saw (Fig. 2-34). Clean up the edge with a small file.

The inner and outer veneer rings must now be scraped or sanded down to a thickness slightly greater than that of the abalone. Put the inner ring back on the gluing form and hold it in place with push pins. Lay the abalone segments in place around the veneer ring and file the ends so that they butt tightly. Now the abalone and veneer rings can be epoxied together and clamped with push pins just as the veneer rings were assembled.

When the epoxy is hard, sand both sides of the rosette smooth on a belt sander using a sharp #120 belt. It is almost impossible to perform this operation with anything but a belt sander. Even so, this is very tricky, since the finished rosette is only about 0.04 inch or 1 mm thick. Great care must be taken not to get the rosette too hot from the friction of the sanding belt because this may break down the glue.

Now, a channel must be cut into the guitar top to receive the rosette. Using a sheet of plywood and clamps, secure the top to a flat working surface. The simplest method to make a channel is to incise the inside and outside diameters with a circle cutter such as the X-Acto cutter shown in Figures 2-35 and 2-36. These cuts should not be deeper than two thirds of the thickness of the top. The wood between the cuts can then be removed with a small chisel. One may find this easier to do if the wood to be removed is cut into several narrow circular bands, using the circle cutter. This permits removing smaller pieces and makes chipping or gouging less likely.

The ideal cutter for this job should have the outside face ground to the outside radius of the rosette and be sharpened on one side only. This will give the cleanest cut and prevent distortion of the circle where it crosses the grain lines. When making the cuts by hand, there is a tendency for the blade of a tool like the X-Acto cutter to follow the grain when the cut crosses the harder wood of the ring at an oblique angle. The X-Acto cutter will do a satisfactory job if cuts are made in a series of very light passes.

The channel cutting operation can be done more quickly and with less risk of error if a router with trammel points is used. The Dremel Moto-Tool can also be used if the router base is modified as in Figure 2-37. The stud which projects upward is a ½-inch diameter spacer from a surplus store, held in place by a machine screw the same diameter as the hole in the spacer. The bracket to which the stud is attached comes with a hole in

2-34 Sawing out abalone segments

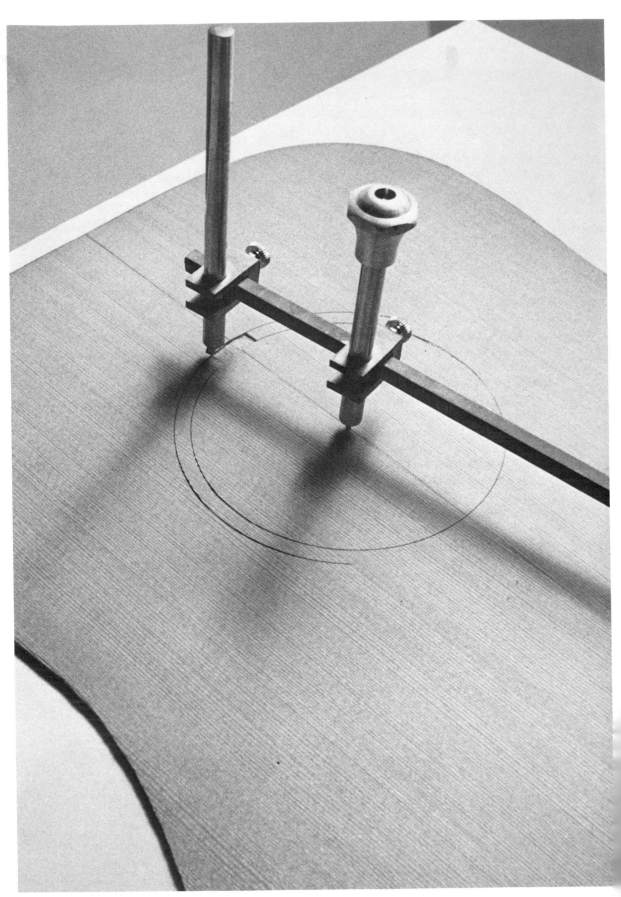

2-35   Cutting recess for rosette

2-36　Method of holding top and cutter

2-37　Modified Dremel router base

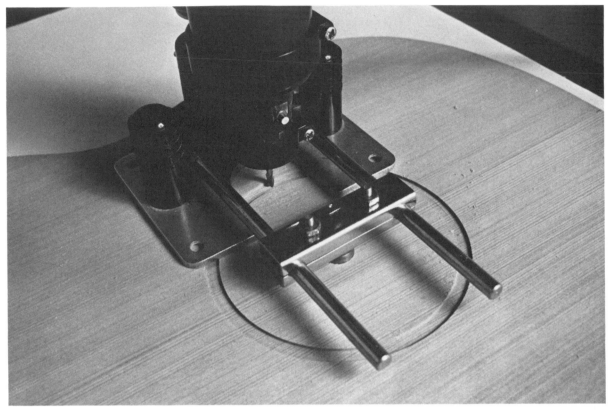

2-38   Dremel setup in use

the appropriate place. Just fasten the pieces together and file off the protruding edges of the nut. Figure 2-38 shows this setup in use.

Standard router bits are satisfactory if they are very sharp. The ideal
cutter is a ¼-inch sheet metal router bit, left hand spiral fluted, right
hand rotation. Since the cut is downward, the problem of tearing out
chips along the edge is minimized. Miniature end mills (⅛-inch diameter)
are available in the forementioned fluting configuration and can be used
with Dremel collets.

A third alternative is to use a router with a standard trammel point attachment. Be sure to get a cutter with a square tip, as sheet metal router
bits often have rounded tips. A ¼-inch straight router bit will do a satisfactory job if sharp.

When drilling the hole in the top for the stud of the trammel points, be
sure the top is securely clamped to the sheet of plywood. Then drill the
appropriate size hole through the top *and* the backup plywood. The stud
will then bear on both pieces rather than just the relatively soft top,

2-39   Cross-section of rosette showing beveled edge for close fit

which could be deformed by the pressure of the rotating stud, thus producing a channel in the top which is not perfectly circular. This can lead to a poorly fitted rosette.

If a ½-inch hole is needed, as shown for the Dremel setup in Figures 2-37 and 2-38, a countersink (power drill type) can be used. Try to cut the

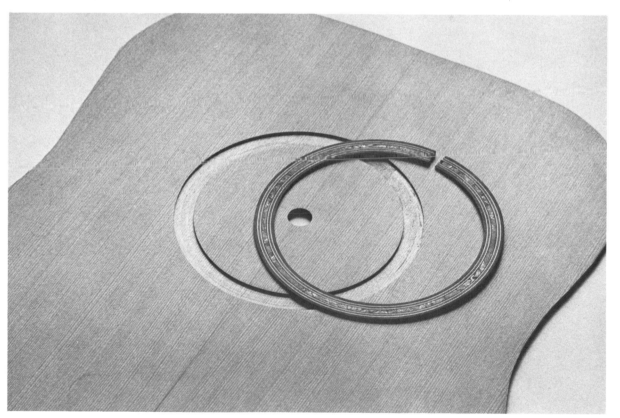

2-40   Rosette ready for gluing

channel just a few thousandths of an inch narrower than the rosette. Final fitting can then be done by scraping or filing the inner and outer black rings slightly.

Bevel the edges of the rosette slightly as in Figure 2-39. Determine the narrowest part of the rosette. They are usually out of round by a few thousandths of an inch. Cut the channel width so that the narrowest part slips in with gentle finger pressure. Figure 2-40 shows an abalone rosette ready for gluing.

Coat the inside of the channel with Titebond (epoxy tends to "bleed" into end grain). Press the rosette gently into place, working excess glue toward the gap at the top of the rosette. Clean off excess glue, place waxed paper over the rosette to prevent sticking, and clamp the rosette with scrap plywood. Leave overnight to dry.

When the glue is completely dry, level the rosette with a scraper or belt sander. Remove the inner circle of wood from the soundhole using the same method by which the rosette channel was cut. If you are using a

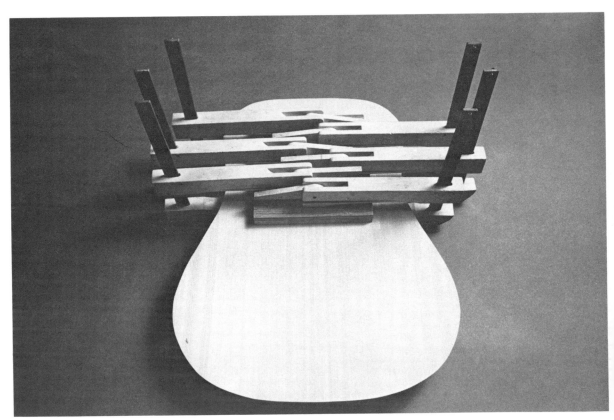

2-41   Rosette glued and clamped

hand cutter, cut halfway through, then turn the top over, and finish the cut from the opposite side.

The top is now ready for bracing.

BRACING AND FITTING THE TOP

After the rosette is inlaid into the top and the soundhole has been cut out, the next step is to lay out the bracing pattern on the top. Using a soft pencil, lightly mark the outline of each brace on the inside of the top, as in Figure 2-42 or 2-43.

BRACING THE TOP

The brace (A) running perpendicular to the center joint (A) is ⅜ inch (9.5 mm) above the edge of the soundhole. The brace is ⅜ inch (9.5 mm) wide; draw both sides of all braces on the top to eliminate any ambiguity in the layout. Measure 1⅝ inches (4.1 cm) down the centerline from the soundhole, and make a mark at that point. Measure ⅝ inch (1.6 cm) down along the perimeter of the top from the bottom side of the brace which was laid out above the soundhole, and mark these two spots. Draw lines connecting each of these marks on the perimeter with the point on the centerline below the soundhole. These lines mark the upper side of the main crossbraces (B and C); draw parallel lines ⅜ inch (9.5 mm) from these lines to mark the other side of the braces. See Figure 2-44 for the profile.

The longer of the two braces (E and F) that cross the center below the reinforcing plate (D) is 3⅛ inch (8 cm) from the right side cross-brace and parallel to it. The other brace is 2 inches (5.1 cm) from the longer brace. Both are ⅜ inch (9.5 mm) wide. See Figure 2-45 for the profile.

The braces (G,H,I,J) which extend from the cross-braces to the sides near the waist (two on each side) are all ¼ inch (6.3 mm) wide. The longer brace (G and I) is 2 ¼ inches (5.7 cm) from the cross-brace it parallels, and the shorter brace (H and J) is 2 inches (5.1 cm) from the longer one. See Figure 2-46 for the profile.

The plate (D) which fits on the inside of the top underneath the bridge prevents the string ends from digging into the soft wood of the top and helps keep the top from being distorted too much by the pull of the strings (see Fig. 2-52). It should be made of maple or rosewood the same thickness as the back. Make it 2 inches wide, with the top edge ¾ inch (1.9 cm) from the joint of the cross-braces (see pattern in Fig. 2-47).

The three braces (K,L,M) around the soundhole are there to keep the top from being distorted in this area by the pull of the strings. They are ¼ inch (6.5 mm) square, and the ends butt tightly against the other braces at the ends. The bottom brace is ⅜ inch (9.5 mm) from the soundhole. The inner margins of the other two braces are 1⅞ inches (4.8 cm)

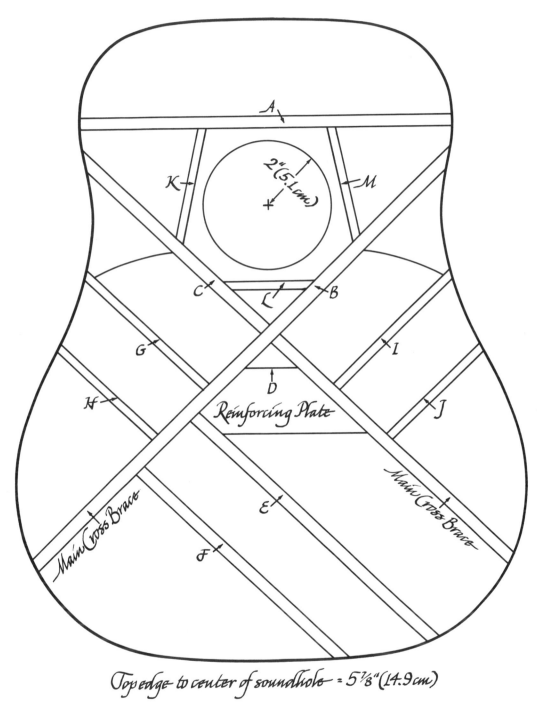

2-42 Six-string top bracing plan

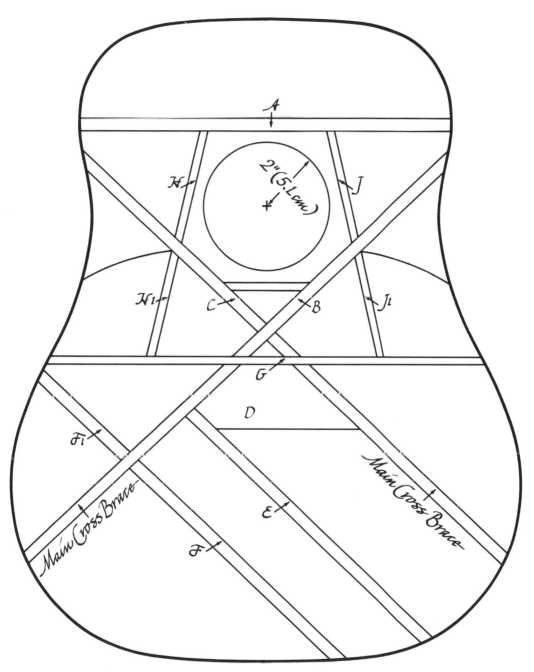

Top edge to center of soundhole = 5⅞" (14.9 cm)

2-43a   Twelve-string top bracing plan

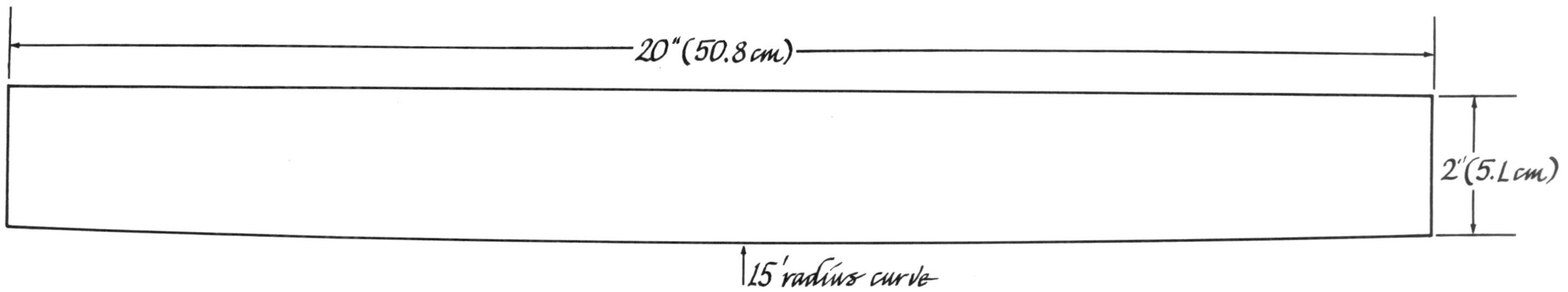

20" (50.8 cm.)

2' (5.1 cm.)

15' radius curve

2-43b   Back arch template

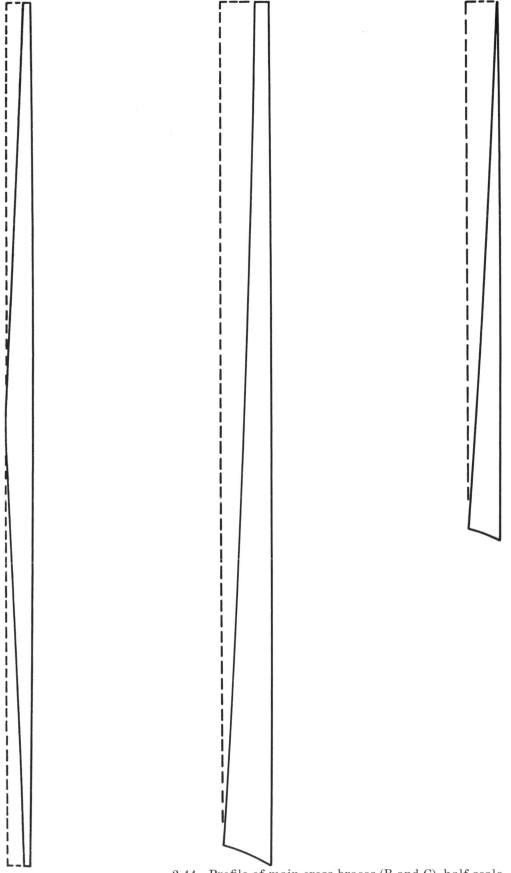

2-44   Profile of main cross-braces (B and C), half-scale

2-45   Bracing profile (E and F), full-scale

2-46   Bracing profile (G, H, I, and J), full-scale

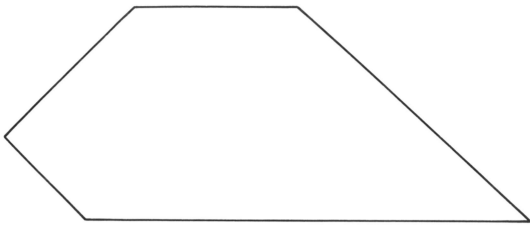

2-47 Bridge reinforcing plate (actual size)

from the centerline at the top and ⅜ inch (9.5 mm) from the soundhole at the nearest point.

Bracing for a twelve-string guitar (Fig. 2-43) is basically the same as for a six-string. The ¼-inch (6.5 mm) wide brace (G) which runs across the width of the top should be fitted into the main cross-braces with a cross-lap joint (see Fig. 2-50), and the height should taper to zero where the brace meets the linings. The ⅜-inch (9.5 mm) wide braces which cross the bottom part of the top should be butted tightly where they intersect the main cross-brace rather than cut away as shown in Figure 2-45, for the six-string. The brace (F) which continues past the cross-brace (B) should be fitted into the cross-brace with a cross-lap joint. The braces (H_1 and J_1) which are a continuation of the soundhole reinforcement should be the same size as the braces around the soundhole and butt tightly at the ends.

ARCHING THE TOP

Although nearly all steel string guitars (other than electric of f-hole types) are built with flat tops, an arched top is superior for several reasons. First, it is stronger, hence less likely to crack either from mishandling or a sudden drop in humidity. An arched top is more stable than a flat top, so the playing action can be set lower without string buzzes appearing whenever the humidity drops. Arching prevents string tension from distorting the top into a severe S-curve, a fairly common problem with old guitars. An arched top has a superior strength-to-weight ratio and produces a more sensitive, louder, more sustained and usually a better balanced tone.

Constructing an arched top is far more work than a flat top, but an arched top is the most important single factor in producing a superior

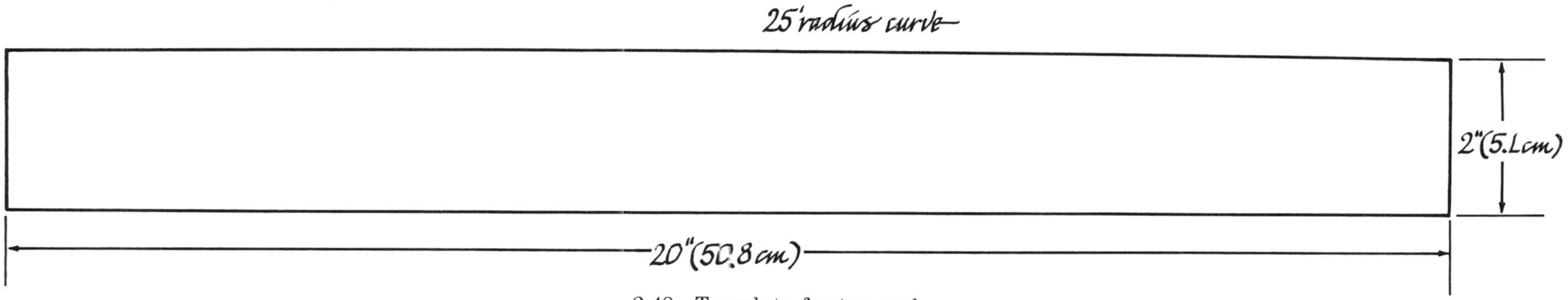

2"(5.1cm)

25' radius curve

20"(50.8cm)

2-48 Template for top arch

guitar. A template is needed for laying out the arch of both top and back. It should be cut from heavy pattern paper or any thin, stiff material.

The curvature of the tops of the guitars in the construction illustrations is spherical, with a 25-foot radius. Using a 25-foot length of wire or light cable (the woven wire sold for hanging pictures is good), draw a 20-inch arc on the template material. Tie one end to any fixed point, and tie a loop in the other end. Insert a sharp pencil through the loop to draw the arc. Now, shorten the cable to 15 feet and draw a 20-inch arc for the back arch template (see Fig. 2-48a). Cut out the templates, taking care to follow the curve accurately.

Using the 25-foot radius template, cut out the braces, using straight, vertical grain spruce for maximum strength (see Fig. 2-48b). All of these spruce braces must be sanded to the correct arch on the bottom surface. Figure 2-49 shows a simple jig for keeping the surfaces perpendicular. The two blocks can be any pieces of scrap wood; the smaller piece must have one straight, perpendicular edge which is used as a fence. Place a

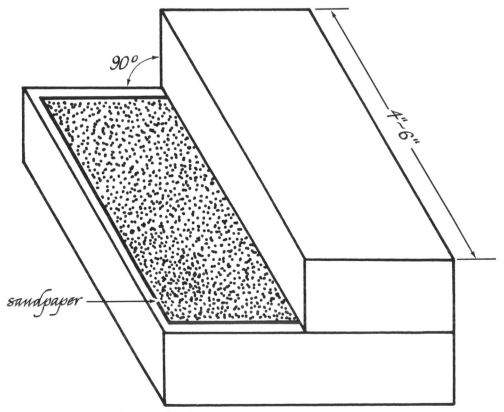

2-49 Sanding jig for arching braces

2-50 Clamping top braces

sheet of 120 grit sandpaper between the two pieces of wood and clamp them in a vise. Rest the side of the brace on the bottom piece and slide the curved surface of the brace back and forth on the sandpaper until the arch conforms to the template.

The cross-brace under the end of the fingerboard should be made of straight, vertical grain mahogany, ³/₈ inch (9.5 mm) thick by ³/₄ inch (1.9 cm) high. This brace must be left flat on the bottom. If it were arched, the strings would be too high at the bridge. It is essential that this brace be as stable as possible, hence the choice of mahogany rather than spruce.

Before gluing on the braces, the top plate can be prearched by exposing the inner side to heat, such as from a hair dryer, or even sunlight. This will dry out the inner surface of the wood and cause cupping. Be careful not to use too much heat (not over about 100°F) or too prolonged exposure, or the top may crack. Properly done, the top will pull itself into an even, approximately spherical curve. Remove the top from the heat when the curve matches the top template. This operation helps stabilize the arch and lessens the likelihood of cracking due to sudden humidity changes.

Glue the braces on as shown in Figure 2-50, using a strip of thin wood under the outer face of the top to protect it from the clamps and a straight piece of one-inch (2.5 cm) square wood over the brace. The top of the brace must be perfectly straight at this point so that the correct arch will be held during gluing.

It is important to use a cross-lap joint where the two main braces cross (see Fig. 2-51). Factory guitars generally use a butt joint reinforced with glue-saturated cloth. This is a weak joint, and loose braces are a fairly common repair problem as a result.

After gluing the cross-braces, glue on the large braces across the bottom center and fit the bridge reinforcement as shown in Figure 2-52.

In order to preserve an accurate and uniform arch, the braces must be planed to their final shape after the glue has dried. The wood in the dotted portions of the profile drawings in Figures 2-44, 2-45, and 2-46 is planed away. The dashed lines represent the profiles before shaping and the solid outlines represent the final profiles of the braces. The mahogany brace (A) which crosses under the fingerboard is rounded off on top then tapered down to ¹/₂ inch (1.3 cm) at the ends.

When all the bracing is glued and shaped, the top will appear as in Figure 2-53.

The sides must now be clamped in the mold so that about ¹/₂ inch of the top edge projects. File or sand the edge of the sides, bottom block, and linings smooth, and bevel them slightly to correspond to the arch in the top. The top block *only* should be left flat, since the mahogany cross-brace is not arched and this upper portion of the top should remain flat.

Lay the braced top in place on the sides, with centerlines matched.

Peghead inlay in mother-of-pearl, abalone, and brass

Rosewood six-string guitar with redwood top

Peghead inlay in mother-of-pearl, abalone, and gold

Rosewood six-string guitar with abalone inlay around top, fingerboard, and peghead

Peghead inlay in mother-of-pearl and gold

Peghead inlay in mother-of-pearl, abalone, ivory, and gold

Rosewood twelve-string guitar

Edge binding and purfling in classic
guitar style

Detail of bridge showing ramps for
strings

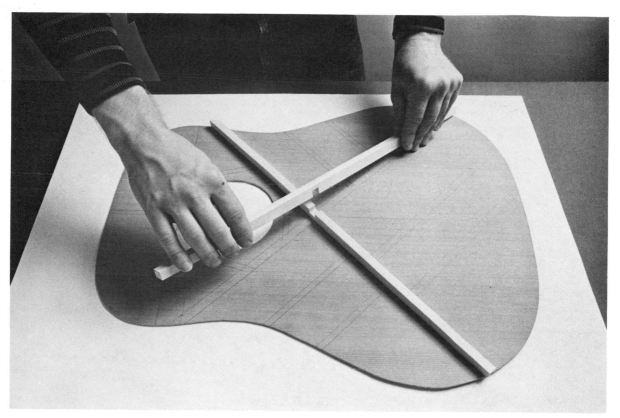

2-51   Cross-lap joint

2-52   Clamping bridge reinforcing plate

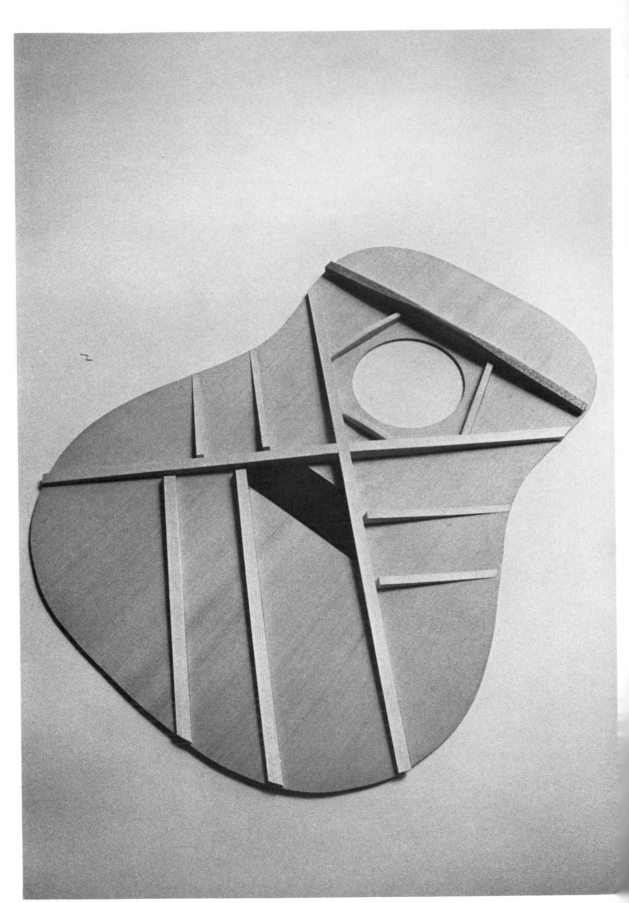

2-53 Braced top

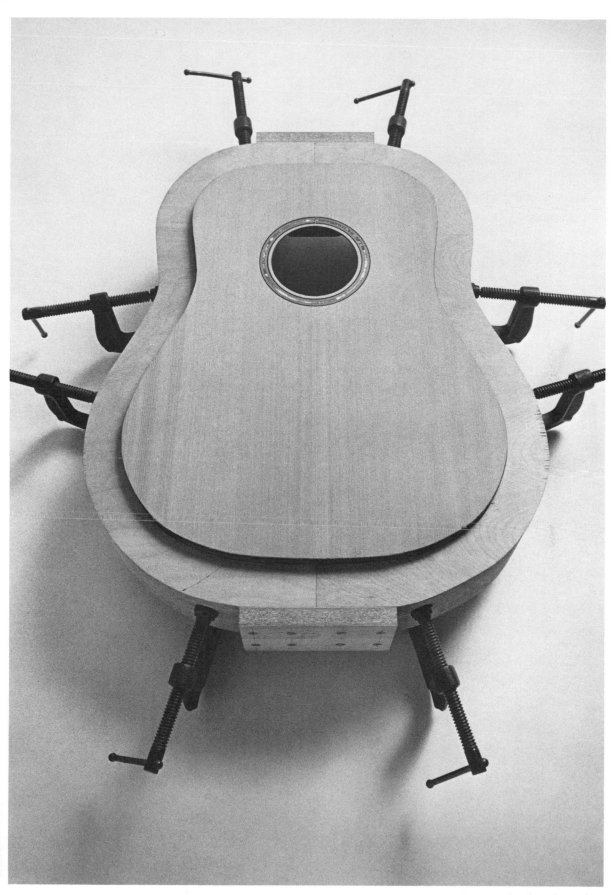

2-54 Top ready for clamping

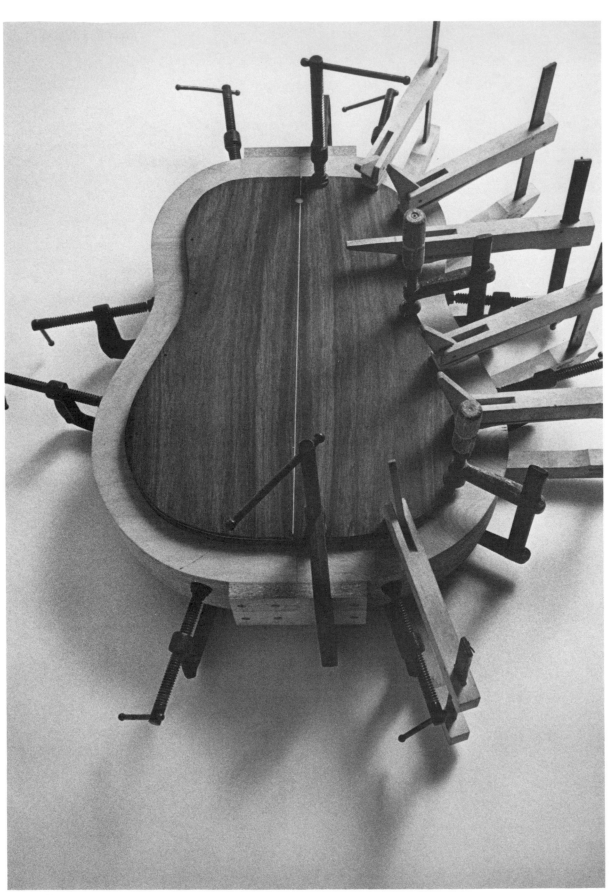

2-55 Top partially clamped

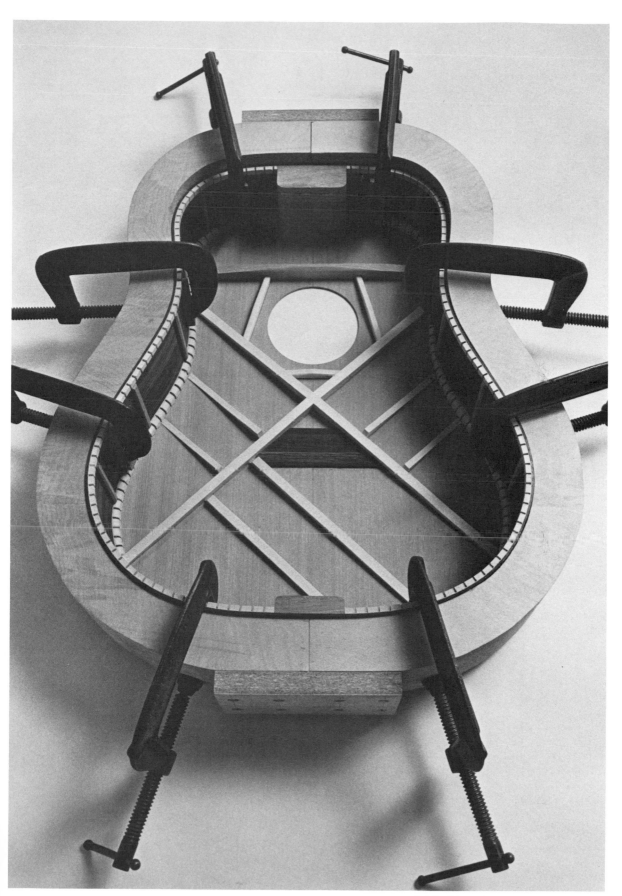

2-56 Top glued on, inside view

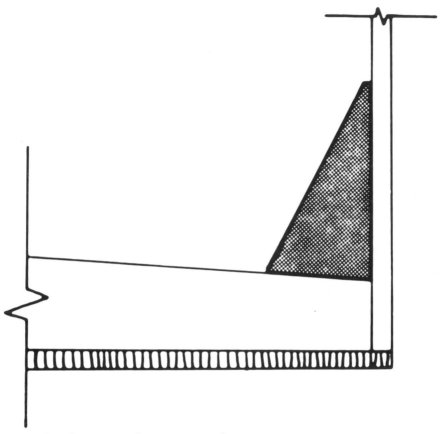

2-57 Brackets on mahogany cross-brace

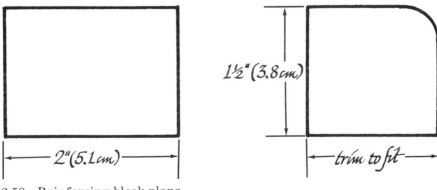

2-58 Reinforcing block plans

2-59 Gluing reinforcing block

2-60 Clamping waist reinforcement

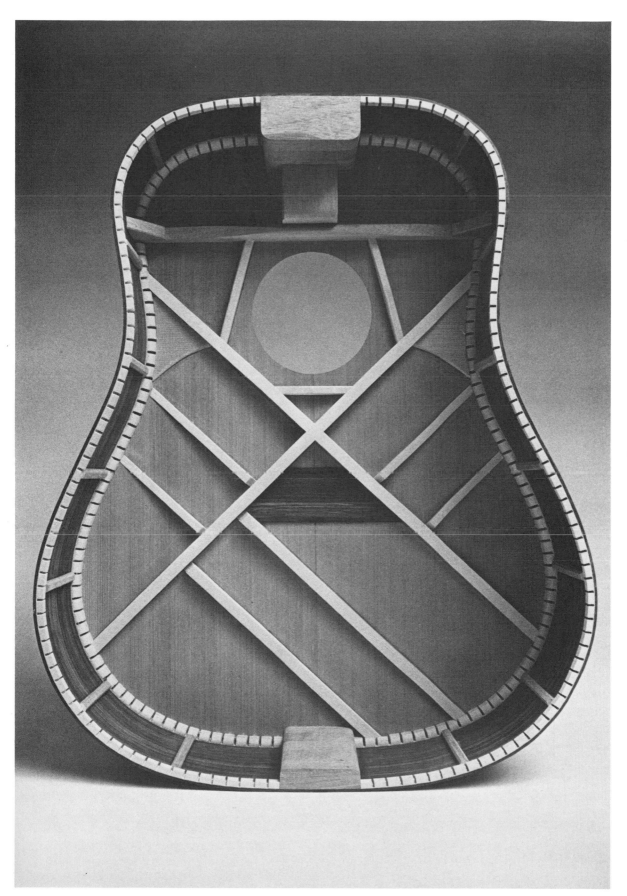

2-61 Top and sides completely assembled

Mark the linings where they touch the mahogany cross-brace and the cross-brace at the inner surface of the sides. Cut away the marked section of linings completely, and trim the cross-brace so that it fits within the sides and slips into the gap in the linings.

Mark the linings where the other braces intersect with them and cut away the linings so that the ends of the braces are held snugly in place when they are trimmed to fit within the sides. Figure 2-54 shows the sides clamped to the mold and the top in place ready for gluing.

Place a sheet of 1/8-inch plywood cut to the outline of the top (or an unbraced back, as in the illustration) over the top to protect it from the clamps. Glue on the top, using Titebond, as shown in Figure 2-55. Figure 2-56 shows the top glued on, after the clamps have been removed.

Before gluing on the back, it is necessary to glue brackets to the ends of the mahogany cross-brace as shown in Figure 2-57. A reinforcing block (Fig. 2-58) is glued between the top block and cross-brace as shown in Figure 2-59. This area bears the load of the string tension on the neck and top, and it is very important to maintain rigidity. Poor design here is a common cause of warped fingerboards and incorrect neck set in factory-made guitars.

A reinforcing plate should be glued in at the waist as shown in Figure 2-60. This is necessary for redwood tops, which are relatively fragile, and is a good idea regardless of what wood is used for the top. The plate should be made of redwood, cedar, or spruce the same thickness as the top. The grain in the reinforcing plate should run perpendicular to the grain of the top. Use a piece of hard wood cut to the shape of the reinforcing plate to distribute the pressure and to protect the soft wood while clamping. Titebond is satisfactory for this joint. Finally, trim off any places where the top overhangs the sides. The sides and completely braced top are shown in Figure 2-61.

BRACING AND FITTING THE BACK

The braces for the back should be made of straight, vertical grain Honduras mahogany, 3/8 inch (9.5 mm) wide by 1/2 inch (1.3 cm) high at the center. See Figure 2-62 for layout dimensions. The dotted lines in Figure 2-62 represent the center panel in a three-piece back. It is 1 1/2 inches (3.8 cm) wide at the top and 5 inches (12.7 cm) wide at the bottom.

Shape the bottom surface of the braces using the 15 foot radius arching template. The back should be as dry as possible before bracing. Gentle heating of the inner surface as previously described is appropriate here, but the denser woods used for the back will not conform to the tighter radius of the back by heating alone. Nevertheless, it is important to have the wood as dry as possible before bracing to minimize the possibility of cracking.

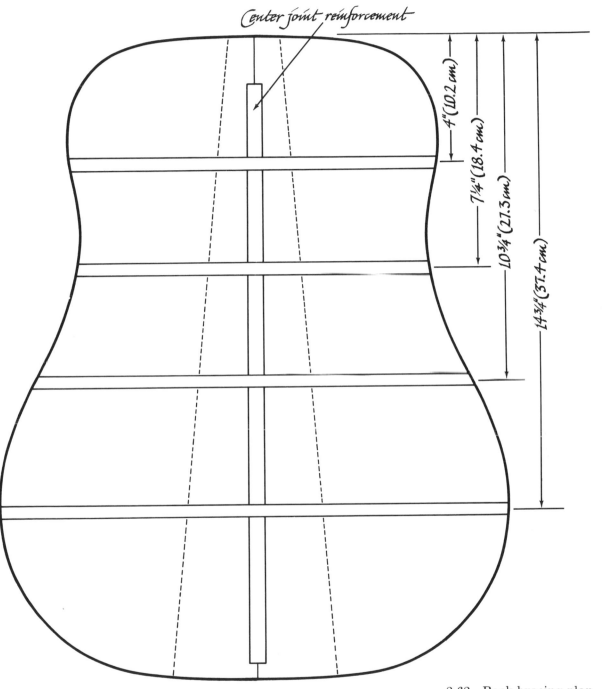

Center joint reinforcement

4" (10.2 cm.)

7¼" (18.4 cm.)

10¾" (27.3 cm.)

14¾" (37.4 cm.)

2-62 Back bracing plan

2-63   Clamping back bracing

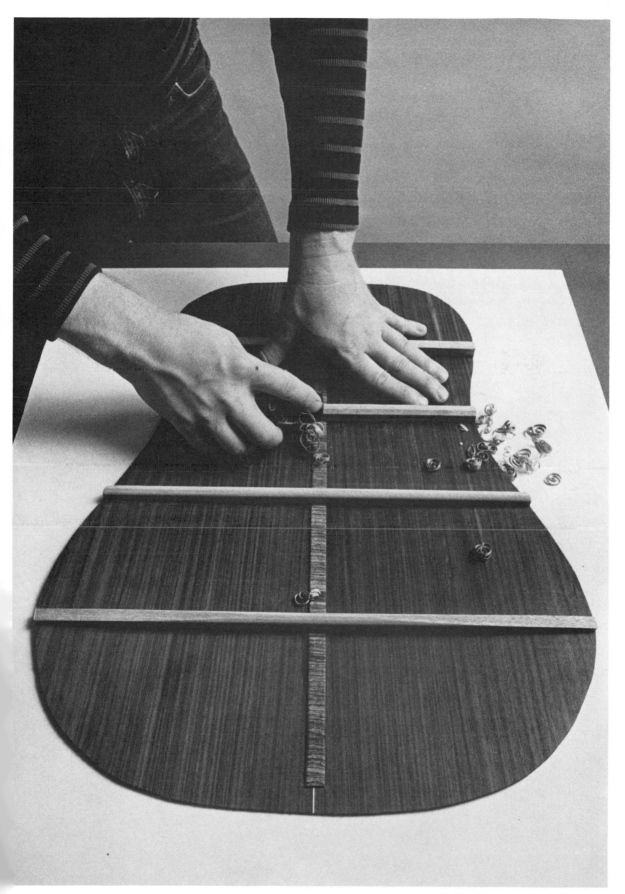

2-64 Shaping back bracing

When you are satisfied that the wood is as dry as possible (don't overdo the heat and crack the wood), glue on the braces as in Figure 2-63. Titebond is adequate for this purpose. Shape the tops of the braces as in Figure 2-64. Round off the tops, then taper the ends to ⅛ inch (3.2 mm).

The center joint (or joints, if you are using a three piece back), must be reinforced by a narrow strip of mahogany or rosewood cut so that the grain runs perpendicular to the grain of the back panels. See Figure 2-65 for the dimensions. This can be done before or after gluing the braces on, whichever you choose.

When bracing and center joint reinforcement are finished, it is time to glue in a label with your name and the date (Fig. 2-66).

Once the back is braced, some preparation is necessary before gluing it to the sides and top. Small blocks must be cut very carefully to fit all around the edge of the top just inside the mold as in Figure 2-67. These blocks compensate for the arch in the top, allowing a flat plate of ¾-inch plywood to be slid under the top to take the pressure of the clamps while gluing on the back. The back could be glued on by clamping directly against the top, but this might crack the top and/or distort the guitar body.

The small blocks must be precisely the right thickness to support the sides uniformly all around the perimeter. They should be about ½ inch (1.3 cm) square at the waist, gradually increasing in depth to about ⅝ inch (1.6 cm) at the top and bottom.

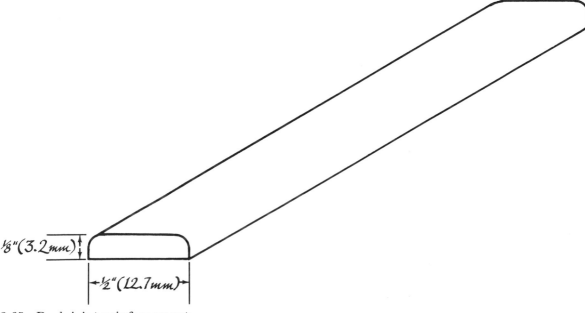

⅛"(3.2mm)

½"(12.7mm)

2-65 Back joint reinforcement

2-66 Completed back with label

The easiest way to graduate the blocks is to clamp the sides in the mold so that the top is about ½ inch from the edge at the waist (see Fig. 2-68). Working with the top facing upward, set the blocks in place around the top and scribe the blocks where they intersect the edge of the mold. Trim the blocks to size and tape them to the side of the mold so they won't be jostled away from the edge and lead to cracks when clamping pressure is applied.

When you are satisfied that the blocks are properly fitted, slip the body into the mold until it rests on the support blocks and prop the waist open so that the sides fit against the mold as shown in Figure 2-69. The tool used in the photograph is a turnbuckle with the eyes cut off the screws; a piece of scrap wood cut to the right length and wedged in will work as well.

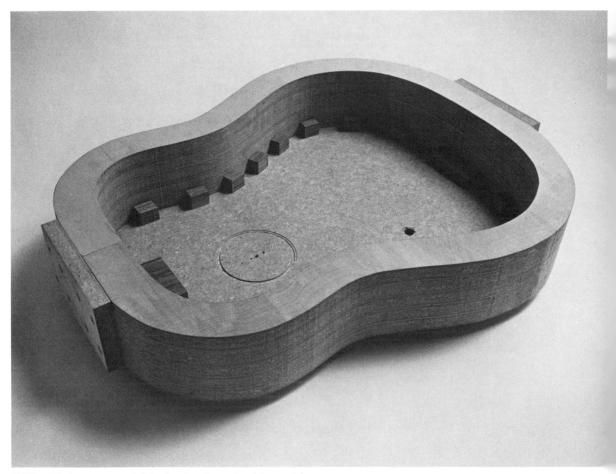

2-67   Gluing support blocks in place inside mold

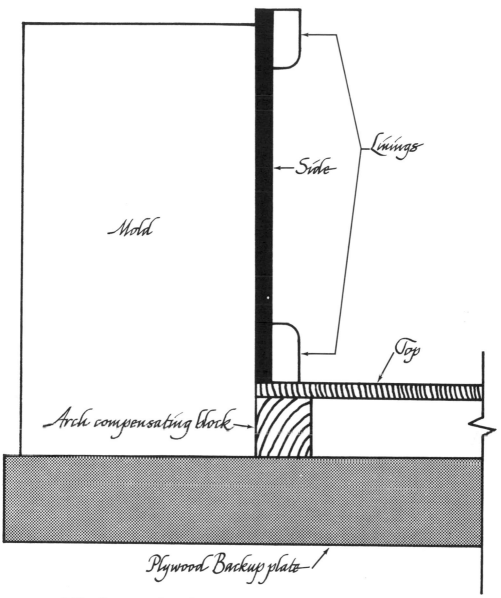

Mold

←Side

Linings

Top

Arch compensating block—

Plywood Backup plate—

2-68 Cross-section of set-up for clamping back to top and sides in mold

Bevel the gluing surface of the linings and end blocks to conform to the curvature of the back, and cut recesses in the linings for the ends of the braces as was done for the top braces.

Glue on the back as shown in Figure 2-70, using Titebond. Protect the back with the same piece of material which was used to protect the top,

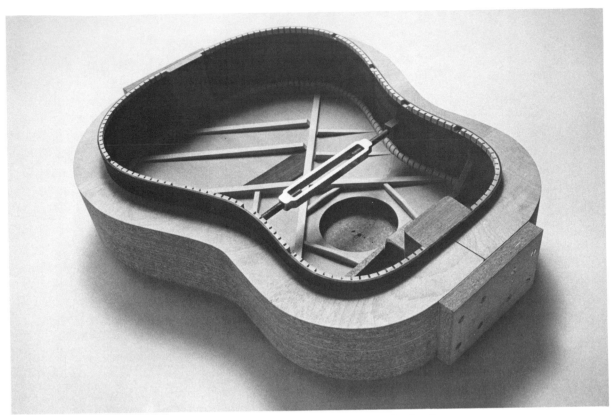

2-69   Top and sides propped in the mold, ready for gluing on the back

2-70   Clamping the back

and place blocks of scrap wood under the clamp pads to distribute the clamping pressure.

MAKING THE EDGE BINDING

A thin strip of wood should be glued around the edges of the guitar body to protect it from accidental blows and to seal the end grain of the top and back.

Mass produced instruments generally use plastic for edge binding, but this material has serious drawbacks. It tends to shrink and become brittle with age and to pull away from the wood at the waist of the guitar. It is difficult to get a really strong glue bond between wood and acetate or celluloid, the plastics most often used for edge binding. Plastic can be glued on quickly without pre-bending, and black and white or colored purfling lines can be molded into the strip. It is possible to glue plastic around all the edges in one operation, thereby saving a great deal of labor. Plastic edges are quick and cheap, but this is all that can be said for them.

It is sometimes said that plastic edges make removal of the top or back easier, should it be necessary for repairs. This is logical if one is thinking of fiddle repair techniques, but guitar construction is radically different. Nearly all repairs which necessitate removing a guitar back are due to faulty design or construction of the instrument. If it had been correctly made in the first place, there would be no need to make such major repairs at all. Plastic edges cause more repair problems than they solve, and they cheapen any instrument.

The simplest wood edge binding is a strip of maple or rosewood, about 1/4" x 1/10" (6.4 mm x 2.5 mm). The novice luthier should use maple for the first guitar, as it is easier to bend and finish.

CUTTING THE EDGE BINDING

The edge binding strips are cut from a 1/4-inch (6.4 mm) thick piece of straight, vertical grain wood, about 32 inches (81 cm) long and usually 3 or 4 inches (7.6 to 10.2 cm) wide. Four strips 1/10 inch (2.5 mm) wide are cut off with a bandsaw or table saw. If you want side purfling, glue a sheet of contrasting veneer to the face of the slab before cutting it into strips (see Fig. 2-71).

These strips must be pre-bent to shape the same way the sides were bent. Don't soak the strips as you did the sides; just dip them in water, allow a few minutes for the water to penetrate, then bend. Re-moisten during bending if necessary. These thin strips are fragile, especially if made of rosewood. If they fracture during bending, it may be possible to salvage the piece by gluing the crack together and clamping with a small C-clamp. Strips broken through should be discarded. With practice, a light touch which will minimize breakage can be developed.

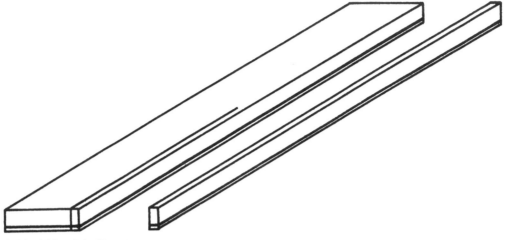

2-71   Edge binding layup (with side purfling)

Before fitting edge binding, scrape or sand the sides to remove overhanging wood from the back or top and to even out the bumps and valleys that tend to appear during bending. This will give the cutting tool an accurate surface to use as a guide when cutting the recess for the edge binding and purfling.

FITTING THE EDGE BINDING

A ledge must be routed around the edges to receive the edge binding and purfling. Cut the top ledge first and glue on the top bindings before cutting the ledge for the back bindings. This will protect the soft top edges from possible damage while fitting the back edges. The ledge can be cut by hand with a violin purfling groove cutter, or with the home-made cutter shown in Figure 1-5. However, the easiest way to accomplish this is by using a shaper table or a router. The shaper table shown in Figure 2-72 was improvised by mounting a router upside down under the table-top. The best cutter is a ¼-inch sheet metal router bit, with right hand rotation, left hand spiral, and square tip (available from industrial supply houses). The left hand spiral reduces chipping. An ordinary straight router bit is adequate, if sheet metal bits are not available.

A shim is needed to compensate for the arch of the top and back (see Fig. 2-73). To make an adjustable guide as shown in Figure 2-72, clamp a block of scrap wood to the tabletop for a fence, and round the end of another piece of scrap for a guide. The guide can be slid back and forth to adjust the width of the cut. Adjust the cutter to the depth of the edge binding, checking by making a cut in a piece of soft scrap wood. The first cutting pass should only be about ¹⁄₃₂ inch deep to avoid chipping. The full

2-72   Guide set-up for improvised shaper table

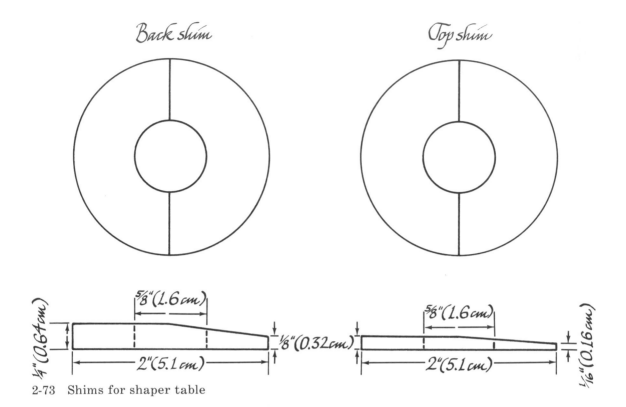

Back shim · Top shim

5/8" (1.6 cm) · 5/8" (1.6 cm)
1/4" (0.64 cm) · 1/8" (0.32 cm) · 1/16" (0.16 cm)
2" (5.1 cm) · 2" (5.1 cm)

2-73 Shims for shaper table

2-74 Cutting recess for edge binding

width should then be cut by moving the guide finger back and checking by cutting first on scrap wood. Figure 2-74 shows this setup in use.

If the purfling on the top is wider than $1/16$ inch, the recess for the purfling should be cut only as deep as the thickness of the top (Fig. 2-75). If wide purfling is fitted the full depth of the edge binding, it is likely to be so stiff that it will crack when bent around the sharp curve at the top bout.

If a router is to be used by hand, some modifications are needed to compensate for the arch in the top and the back. A guide finger is usually included with the trammel points accessory. The contact surface of the guide should be bent as shown in Figure 2-76 to keep the guide point close to the cutter and to help compensate for the tilting of the router due to the arch of the top and back. The base plate of the router should be

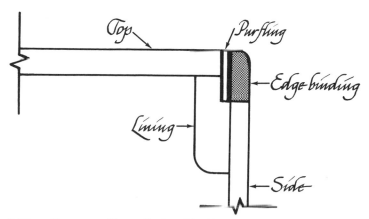

2-75a   Cross-section of edge binding with narrow purfling

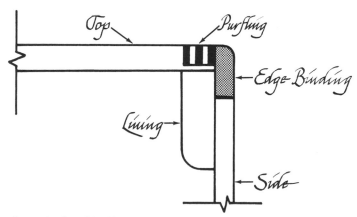

2-75b   Cross-section of edge binding with step-cut ledge for wide purfling

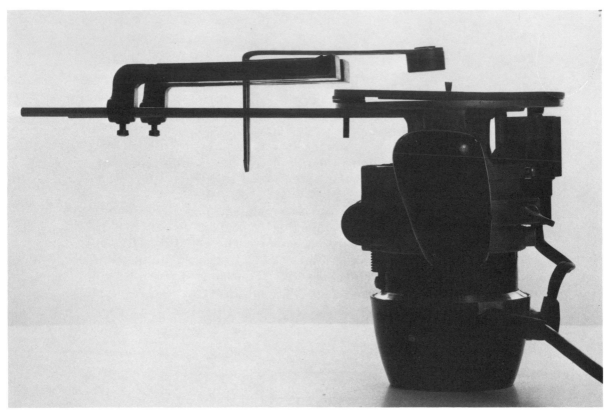

2-76　Set-up for hand router

2-77　Cutting edge binding recess by hand

shimmed with washers as shown in Figure 2-76 to compensate for the arch.

Cutting the recess is done in the same way as with a shaper table. Adjust the cutter to the proper depth and make a $\frac{1}{32}$-inch wide cut, then adjust the cut to full width and complete the full cut. Always check the adjustments on scrap wood before making the actual cut. It is necessary to have someone hold the body while using a hand-held router.

The procedure for using a hand cutter is basically the same. Adjust the cutter to the proper width and make a cut about $\frac{1}{16}$ inch deep (Fig. 2-77). Remove the waste with a sharp $\frac{1}{4}$-inch chisel (Fig. 2-78). Repeat this procedure until the edge is completely cut.

Before fitting, the edge binding should be bevelled slightly to ensure a tight fit (Fig. 2-79). Scrape the inner surface to clean any residue from bending and to ensure a good glue joint. Tape purfling in place at one edge and check the fit all around; it may be necessary to true up the ledge slightly in spots, especially around the top bout. Mark the ends of the

2-78   Removing waste wood

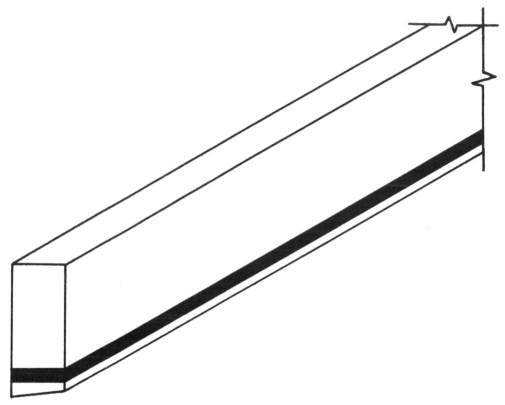

2-79 Bevelling edge binding

binding and purfling to the correct length and trim. Be very careful when removing tape from spruce, as it is very easy to tear out long slivers of summerwood by ripping the tape off quickly.

When gluing on an edge, it is necessary to protect the opposite side recess, otherwise the cord used for clamping on the edges will dig into the ledge. Plastic functions magnificently in this capacity. Nylon is ideal, since it will not stick to glue, but acetate is satisfactory. Make the strip the same size in cross-section as the edge binding, and cut it about ½ inch (1.3 cm) shorter than the actual edge binding so there will be room at each end for cleaning excess glue from the recess. A strip of maple or rosewood can be substituted, but it will have to be pre-bent to shape.

Starting at the bottom, glue up about one third of the edge and purfling with Titebond and tape the edge binding in place. (It is impossible to clamp the whole perimeter evenly at one time.) Wipe away excess glue and tie the edge binding firmly in place by wrapping with parachute line, sash cord, or 3/16-inch shock cord (Fig. 2-80). A 100-foot length is necessary.

2-80 Tying edge binding and back purfling in place

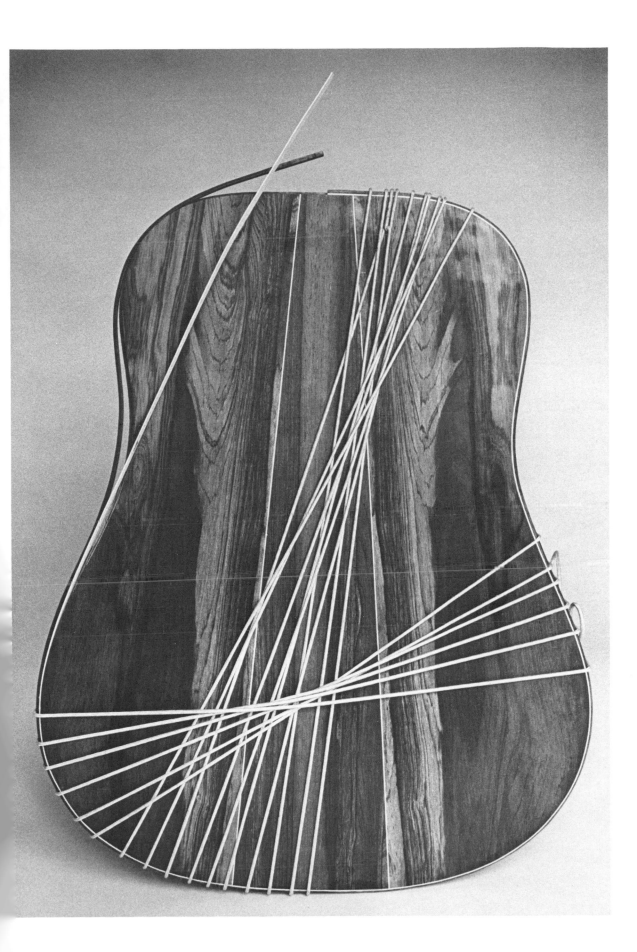

Shock cord has a woven sheath around a rubber strand core; this is ideal, but somewhat expensive.

When all the edges are glued on, trim off any overhang and round them off so there will be no sharp edges digging into the player's arms or legs. Rounded edges also take lacquer better.

Drill a hole in the center of the bottom wedge and fit the end pin (Fig. 2-81). Wooden end pins are tapered and require a violin peg reamer for fitting. This is a rather expensive tool, so you may elect to use a metal end pin which is held in place with a screw.

2-81   Fitting the end pin

3 The Neck, Fingerboard & Bridge

MAKING THE NECK

Due to the high tension of steel strings, some sort of reinforcement is necessary to prevent the neck from being warped. The usual approach is to embed a steel truss rod in the neck, with one end anchored near the heel and the other end extending to the peghead just past the nut. The end of the rod is threaded, and tightening the hex nut (under the cover plate screwed to the peghead) puts tension on the rod which counterbalances the tension of the strings. Unfortunately this doubles the compression load on the neck and tends to warp the neck into an s-curve.

A more sound solution is to embed a solid $1/4''$ x $1/2''$ steel bar into the neck so that the $1/2$-inch dimension is perpendicular to the fingerboard. There is no advantage to using any material other than steel, or any exotic steel alloys, since stiffness rather than tensile strength is the relevant variable. There is no advantage to using T or I-shaped beams; they are less stiff than a solid bar of the same overall dimensions. This steel bar produces a very stiff neck which is able to resist the pull of the strings without imposing any additional stress.

The neck and heel should be cut from a piece of straight, vertical grain mahogany $11/16$ inch (1.7 cm) thick, 3 inches (7.6 cm) wide, and 28 inches (71 cm) long. Cut a 7 inch (18 cm) piece off of one end, making the cut at a 15° angle (see the bottom and middle illustrations, Fig. 3-1). For a twelve-string, cut off an $8^{1}/_{2}$ inch (21.6 cm) piece. The cut surfaces must be planed or sanded smooth and flat, then glued together with epoxy as in the top position illustrated in Figure 3-1. Clamp the two pieces, on edge, to the workbench before clamping the glue joint. This will keep the joint from slipping under pressure. When the glue is completely set, plane or sand the surface of the peghead level. Trim the fingerboard portion of the neck to $14^{3}/_{8}$ inches (36.5 cm), and save the remainder to laminate for the heel.

A groove $1/2$ inch deep by $1/4$ inch wide must now be routed down the center of the neck blank to accommodate the reinforcing bar. This is most easily done on a shaper table, but it can be done with a hand-held router.

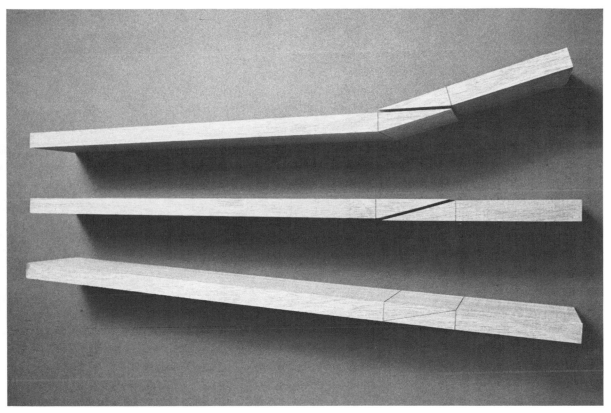

3-1 Peghead splice joint

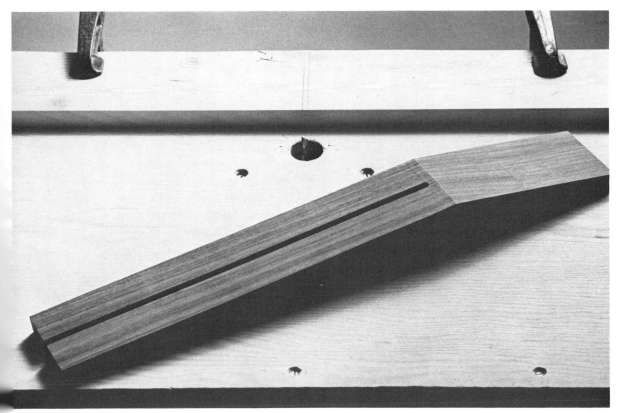

3-2 Routing the slot for the reinforcing bar

3-3 Aligning the peghead veneer

3-4 The peghead veneer is clamped on, then the square is removed to allow
cleanup of excess glue

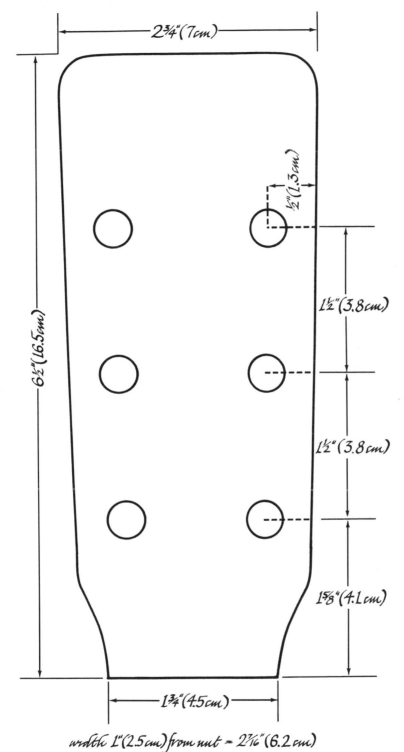

width 1″(2.5 cm) from nut = 2⁷⁄₁₆″(6.2 cm)

3-5   Peghead plan, six-string guitar

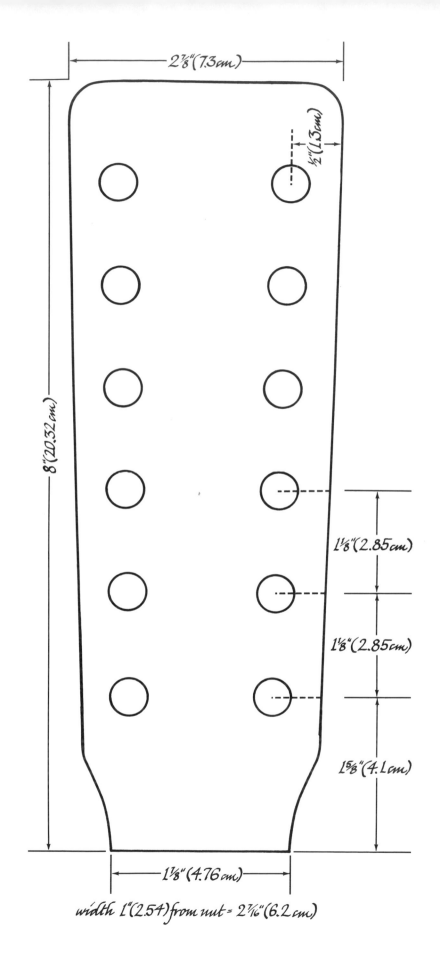

2⅞" (7.3cm)

½" (1.3cm)

8" (20.32cm)

1⅛" (2.85cm)

1⅛" (2.85cm)

1⅝" (4.1cm)

1⅛" (4.76cm)

width 1" (2.54) from nut = 2⅜" (6.2cm)

The groove should end ³⁄₈ inch (.95 cm) before the peghead begins (see Fig. 3-2).

The next step is to glue on the peghead veneer. This is usually rosewood, about ¹⁄₁₀ inch (2.5 cm) thick. If the peghead is to be inlaid, ebony should be used as it shows the inlay to greater advantage and cuts more cleanly. Before gluing, the end which will bear against the nut should be beveled so that it is perpendicular to the face of the neck. It can be aligned for gluing by clamping a straight edge across the end of the peghead to hold the overlay in place (see Fig. 3-3). Use epoxy for this joint, and clamp as in Figure 3-4.

Scribe the fingerboard and peghead outlines and cut them out with a coping saw or bandsaw. See Figures 3-5 and 3-6 for peghead dimensions. The easiest way to lay out the fingerboard outline is to cut out the fingerboard as described in the following chapter and clamp it in place on the neck blank. The outline can be scribed with a knife. Extend the line to the edge of the peghead veneer to get the proper dimension for the nut width and for the narrow end of the peghead. Cut the fingerboard portion about

3-7 Binding the peghead

-6 Peghead plan, twelve-string guitar

$\frac{1}{16}$ inch (1.6 mm) outside the lines. This allows for final alignment when the "set" of the neck is determined.

Drill the holes for the tuning machines, preferably with a drill press.

You may wish to bind the edge of the peghead. This can be done by routing a ledge using the same tool or setup that was employed for fitting the edge binding. The binding in Figure 3-7 is a thin strip of holly veneer bordered by black fiberboard of the type used for violin purfling. Use epoxy for this joint, as you may need its long working time to tie on the binding before the glue sets.

The peghead must be thinned to $\frac{5}{8}$ inch (1.6 cm) to properly accommodate most tuning machines. This can be done with a scraper or by using a router bit in a drill press as shown in Figure 3-8. Adjust the depth of cut by moving the drill table. Take light cuts and be careful to keep the top of the peghead firmly against the work table.

There is a tendency for the metal washer on the tuning machines to blister the lacquer around it when the collar on the tuning machine is tight-

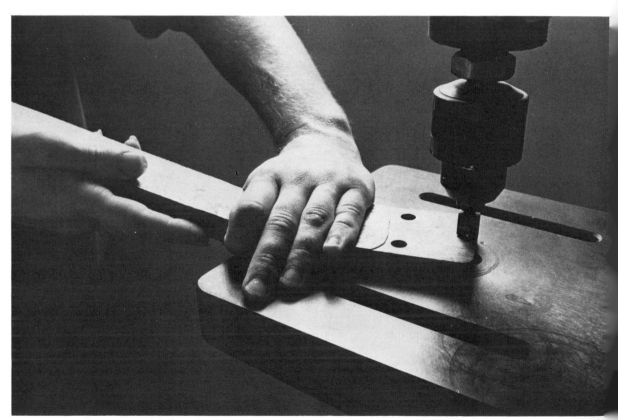

3-8   Thinning the peghead

3-9   Set-up for recessing washer

ened. This can be circumvented by cutting a ½-inch diameter recess for a second washer, so that the pressure of the washers bears on unfinished wood. The recess can be cut on a drill press by clamping a piece of scrap wood to the work table and drilling it through with the same drill used for the holes for the tuning machines. Remove the drill and tape it in the hole so that the blunt end projects ⅛ inch, and chuck a ½-inch end mill in the drill press (Fig. 3-9). The end of the drill will hold the peghead in register while the ¹⁄₁₆-inch deep ledge is cut, as in Figure 3-10.

Figure 3-11 shows the steps in shaping the peghead; the neck on the right has a thin strip of abalone inlaid around the binding.

Using the patterns in Figure 3-12, cut out the heel sections and glue them together, using epoxy. The heel can be made in one piece if you can find mahogany in large enough dimensions. When set, glue the heel to the neck using epoxy again (Fig. 3-13). Drill a ¼-inch hole through the bottom of the reinforcing bar slot two-thirds of the way through the heel and cut a dowel the same length. The dowel will be glued in when the fingerboard

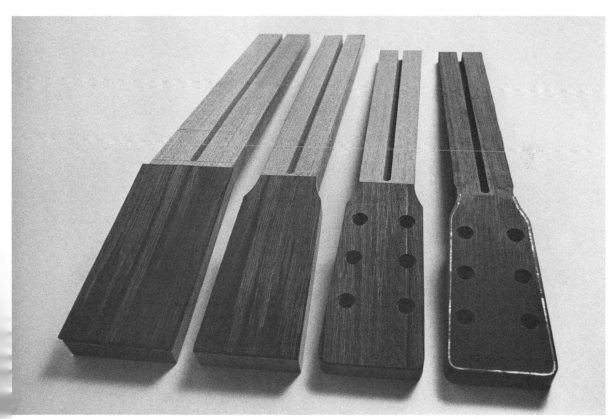

3-11   Steps in shaping the peghead

3-10   Set-up in use for recessing washers

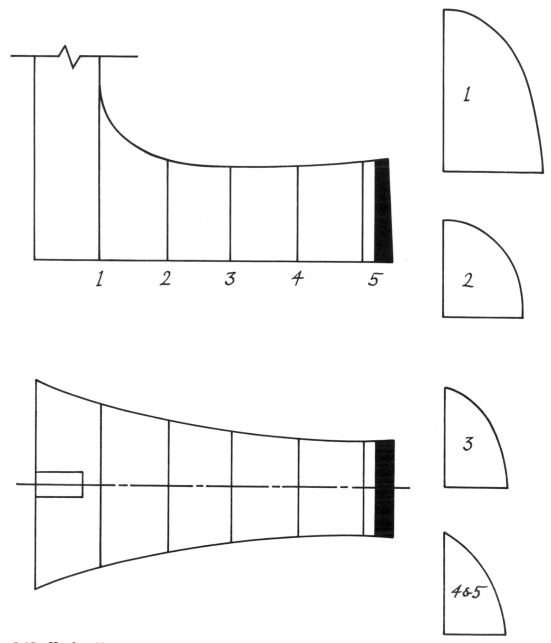

3-12   Heel patterns

3-13 Gluing on heel

is glued to the neck, but the fingerboard must be cut to shape and the neck fitted to the body first.

MAKING THE FINGERBOARD

If you are building your first guitar, you should use rosewood for the fingerboard. It is much easier to work with than ebony, more available, cheaper, and less likely to crack. Ebony fingerboards should be aged before use, if possible for several years.

The first step is to thin the fingerboard to ¼ inch (6.4 mm) and plane or joint one edge perfectly straight. This straight edge is needed for laying out the frets and marking the final shape of the fingerboard. A square and an 18-inch steel rule are needed for laying out the fret positions (see Fig. 3-14). The cheapest way to get a sufficiently accurate and stable straight edge is to buy an 18″ x 1″ x ¼″ dimension ground steel bar from an industrial supply house. This will cost about one-fourth the price of a machinist's straight edge.

3-14 DISTANCE FROM NUT TO FRETS

Fret	Nearest 1/64″	Nearest 1/100″	Nearest 1/10 mm
1	1²⁷⁄₆₄	1.42	36.1
2	2⁴⁹⁄₆₄	2.77	70.5
3	4³⁄₆₄	4.04	92.5
4	5¹⁶⁄₆₄	5.25	102.6
5	6²⁴⁄₆₄	6.38	133.4
6	7²⁹⁄₆₄	7.45	162.1
7	8³⁰⁄₆₄	8.46	215.9
8	9²⁷⁄₆₄	9.42	239.3
9	10²¹⁄₆₄	10.32	262.1
10	11¹¹⁄₆₄	11.17	283.7
11	11⁶²⁄₆₄	11.98	304.3
12	12⁴⁷⁄₆₄	12.72	323.1
13	13²⁸⁄₆₄	13.43	341.1
14	14⁷⁄₆₄	14.11	358.4
15	14⁴⁸⁄₆₄	14.75	374.7
16	15²³⁄₆₄	15.35	389.9
17	15⁵⁹⁄₆₄	15.92	404.4
18	16²⁹⁄₆₄	16.45	417.8
19	16⁵⁹⁄₆₄	16.96	430.8
20	17²⁸⁄₆₄	17.44	443.0

Carefully scribe the fret locations onto the fingerboard, using a sharp knife. Using a fine tooth backsaw with a 0.025 inch (0.635 mm) wide blade (measured across the set of the teeth), cut the fret slots about 1/10 inch (2.5 mm) deep. Use a square to guide the saw and keep the cuts perpendicular to the edge of the board. One saw which meets these specifications is Pennsylvania Saw Corporation® #118.

Draw a centerline down the board with a sharp pencil, and mark the correct width at the nut and twelfth fret with a sharp knife (Fig. 3-15). Scribe the outline of the fingerboard and cut it out. The easiest way is to cut slightly outside the scribe lines and true up the edges by taking very light cuts on a jointer. This gives good control and ensures a straight edge.

Next, set position markers into the edge of the fingerboard as shown in Figure 3-16. The most satisfactory material is gold wire, or a nontarnishing gold or silver substitute available from jewelers and lapidary suppliers. Drill a hole about 1/8 inch (3 mm) into the edge and set the wire in place with epoxy cement dyed black with a small amount of black tinting color (lampblack) or black resin coloring medium, available at paint stores. File the wire ends flush with the edge of the fingerboard when the epoxy has set.

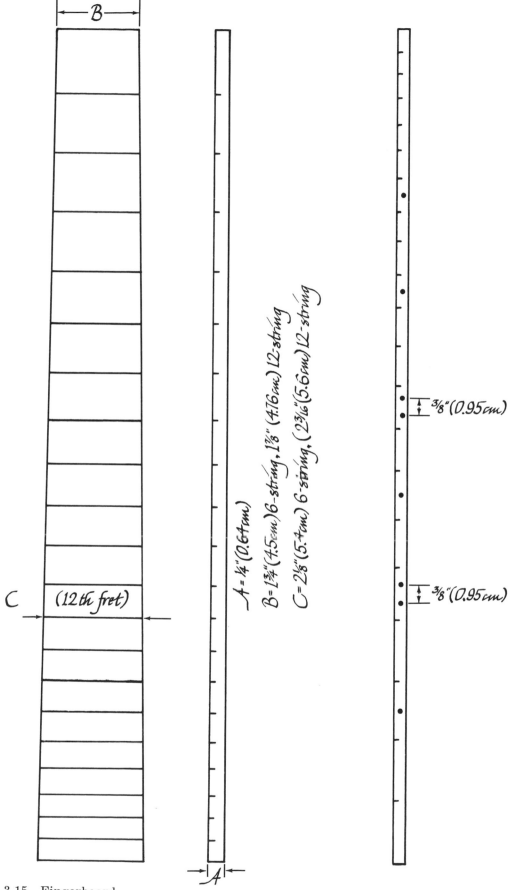

A = ¼" (0.64 cm.)

B = 1¾" (4.5 cm.) 6-string, 1⅞" (4.76 cm.) 12-string

C = 2⅛" (5.4 cm.) 6-string, (2³/₁₆" (5.6 cm.) 12-string

(12th fret)

B

C

A

3/8" (0.95 cm.)

3/8" (0.95 cm.)

3-15 Fingerboard

3-16 Position markers

FITTING THE NECK TO THE BODY

One of the most critical operations in building a guitar is aligning or "setting" the neck. The angle of the neck determines the string height at the bridge, and this dimension must be accurate within 1/8 inch (3.2 mm), preferably plus or minus 1/16 inch (1.6 mm). If the strings are too low at the bridge, picks or fingers will tend to hit the top during playing. If the strings are too high, a very heavy, thick bridge will be needed to keep the saddle height reasonable and the sound of the guitar will suffer.

The easiest way to adjust the set of the neck is to use a bench type belt sander with a tilt table: by clamping a piece of wood to the tilt table and using it as a fence, very good control of the neck angle can be obtained (see Fig. 3-17). Another method is to use a miter box, holding the neck in position by using small wood wedges. The neck set can also be cut with a hand-held belt sander, but this is a bit risky and takes a very steady hand.

Steel string guitar necks are traditionally joined to the body with a dovetail joint, but this is no longer necessary with modern epoxies. The argument that a dovetail makes disassembly for repair easier is, like plastic edges, an example of tinker-toy design philosophy. The only neck joints that the author has seen fail have been dovetail joints.

To determine the proper set for the neck, draw a centerline down the top of the guitar with a soft pencil and make a mark 11½ inches (29.2 cm) from the edge where the neck will be attached. Lay the fingerboard on top of the body just as it will be when the pieces are assembled: the 14th fret should line up with the edge of the guitar body, and the 15th through 20th frets should lie between the edge of the guitar and the soundhole. Place the 18 inch straight edge on top of the fingerboard so that it projects out over the soundhole and measure the distance between the straight edge and the surface of the top at the point 11½ inches down the centerline where the mark was made (see Fig. 3-20). This should be about 1/4 inch (6 mm), plus or minus about 1/16 inch (1.6 mm). If the distance is greater than 5/16 inch (8 mm), taper the fingerboard from the fourteenth fret to the end as in Figure 3-18. Slowly increase the taper until the measurement for the bridge height is correct. If the measurement is less than 3/16 inch (5 mm), the easiest way to correct the problem is to use a thicker fingerboard or add a layer of veneer between the fingerboard and the neck. If the directions for constructing the body have been carefully followed, this measurement should be close to the acceptable limits.

When the proper angle has been determined, clamp the fingerboard to the body and check the neck against the resulting angle to see how much trimming is necessary. Adjust the set of the neck as described above.

Clamp the fingerboard to the neck, leaving 3/16 inch (5 mm) between the peghead and fingerboard to accommodate the nut. Clamp the neck and

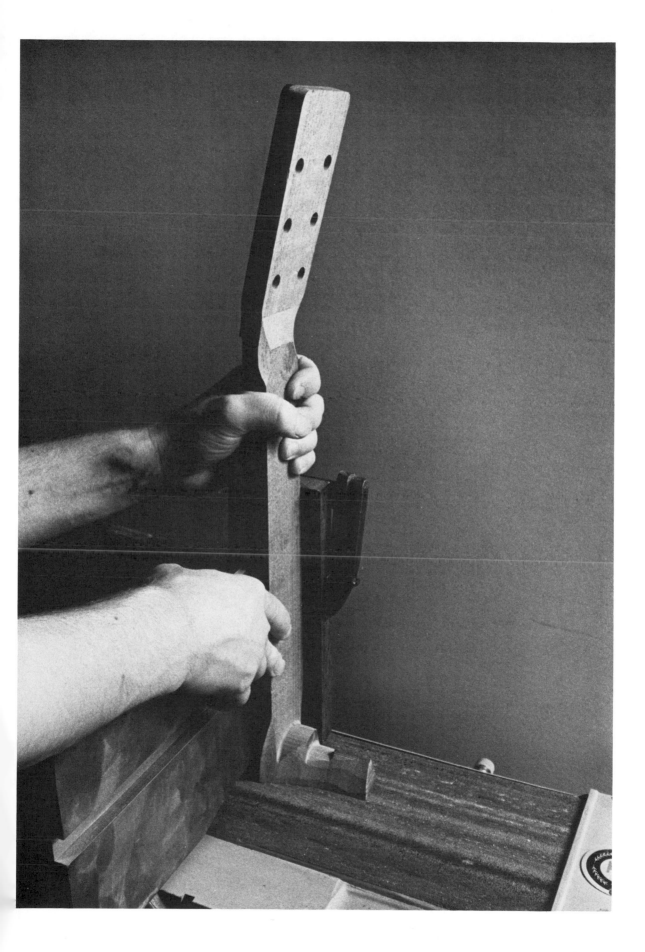

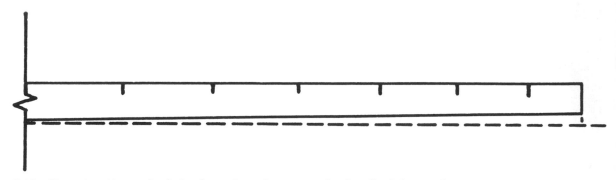

3-18   Tapering the end of the fingerboard to vary the "set" of the neck

fingerboard to the body as in Figure 3-19, and double check the set and alignment of the neck (see Fig. 3-20). Drill through the fret slots at the 1st, 13th, and 15th frets and pin the pieces together with one-inch 18-gauge brads. These will keep the parts lined up during gluing. A brad with the head cut off can be used as a drill to ensure a tight fit.

3-19   Clamping the neck to check for proper "set"

3-20 Checking the neck for proper "set"

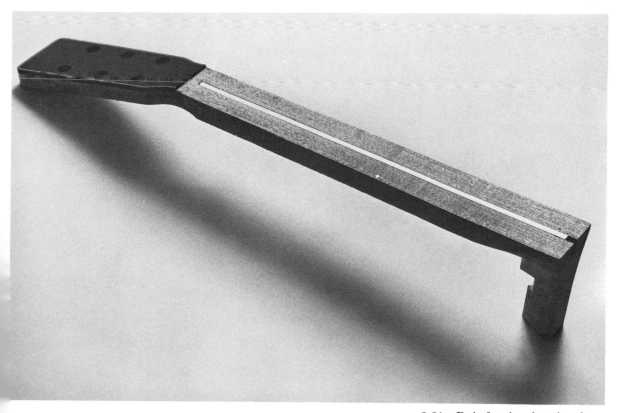

3-21 Reinforcing bar in place

Mark the fingerboard where it crosses the inner margins of the rosette, and trim off the excess wood. Cut the reinforcing steel bar so it fits the slot in the neck with ¼ inch (6 mm) to spare at the heel end (see Fig. 3-21). Using epoxy, glue the dowel into the heel, and set the steel bar into the slot. Coat the brads with soap so the epoxy will not stick to them, and glue on the fingerboard as shown in Figure 3-22, using strips of scrap wood to protect the fingerboard. Wipe away excess glue, being especially careful in the nut groove and where the heel joins the fingerboard.

Shaping the neck is made easier by clamping it to the edge of a workbench, as shown in Figure 3-23. The most efficient shaping tools are a Surform®, rotary rasp, 1-inch drum sander, and double-pointed half-round rasp. A Surform is much easier to use than a spokeshave and cuts closer to the tight curves at the heel and peghead. Shape the heel and the transition from the peghead to the neck first. Then rough out the shape of the neck with the Surform.

Next, thin the neck to ⅞ inch (2.2 cm) overall. An easy way to do this is

3-23 Shaping the neck

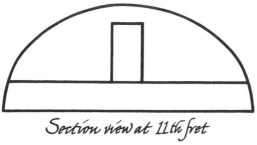

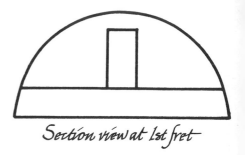

3-24 Neck shape templates, six-string guitar

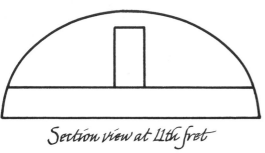

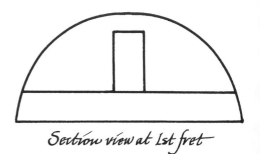

3-25 Neck shape templates, twelve-string guitar

to use a router bit in a drill press. Adjust the table to ⅞ inch (2.2 cm) from the cutter, and push the neck under. Use both hands and take small cuts; this is not as frightening as it sounds. Draw a centerline on the back of the neck and shape according to Figures 3-24 and 3-25. Shape the heel as shown in Figure 3-26.

Clamp the neck in place on the body of the guitar and mark the heel where it crosses the inner margin of the edge binding. Trim off the heel to allow for the heel cap. Fasten a screw eye in the end of the heel and cut a block of scrap wood to the shape shown in Figure 3-27. This specific shape will distribute the clamping pressure as evenly as possible over the area being glued.

Glue the neck on with epoxy as in Figure 3-28. Coat the brads used to hold the fingerboard in position with soap so they can be easily removed. Tie a piece of ⅛ inch (3.2 mm) cord to the end pin, loop it through the screw eye on the heel and tie it with a rolling hitch (see Fig. 3-29). This knot will slip in one direction only. Pull the line tight and slide the knot as snug as it will go. Then slide blocks of scrap wood or small boxes under the line and use these to put more tension on the line (Fig. 3-30).

3-26 Shaping the heel with a drum sander

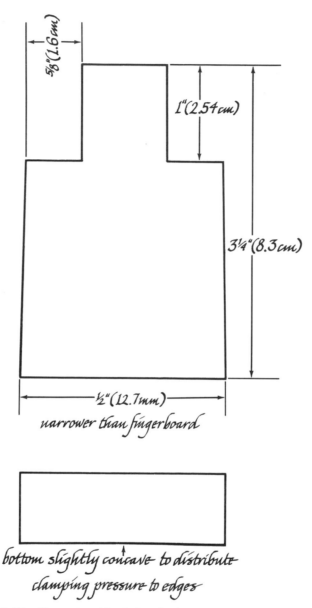

5/8"(1.6cm)

1"(2.54cm)

3¼"(8.3cm)

½"(12.7mm)
narrower than fingerboard

bottom slightly concave to distribute
clamping pressure to edges

3-27 Clamping block for fitting neck

Epoxy can be wiped off completely after the clamp is tightened. When the glue has set, cut the heel cap out of the same material as the fingerboard and glue on as in Figure 3-31. The block of scrap wood under the clamp pad helps keep the heel cap from rotating when the clamp screw is tightened.

3-28 Clamping fingerboard to top

FRETTING

Before fretting, the fingerboard must be straightened and fingerboard inlays (if any) must be set into the surface. The simplest inlays are pearl dots, which are available precut. Any pattern of inlays is permissible, but the layout in Figure 3-32 represents a logical, fairly standard design.

Pencil a centerline down the fingerboard and locate the dots with a small amount of glue. Scribe around the dots with an awl or heavy needle, and lift them off the fingerboard with a razor blade. Rout the holes for the pearl dots with a Dremel Moto-Tool or small dental chisel. A drill can be used for round holes, but it is difficult to keep an ordinary drill bit from wandering off center or cutting too deep.

Fix the pearl dots in place with epoxy cement dyed black with a small amount of lampblack or resin coloring medium.

The most important tool for leveling the neck is a good 18-inch metal straight edge. Using a flat, wooden sanding block about 8 inches long,

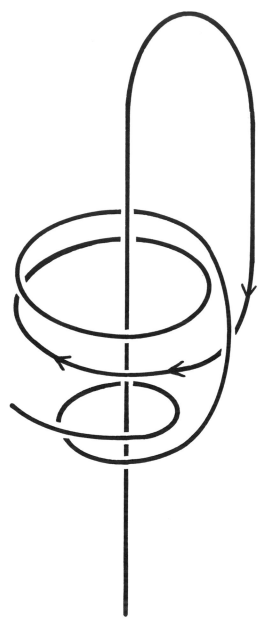

3-29   Rolling hitch

finish the surface of the fingerboard so that it is arched back as shown in Figure 3-33. This is a fairly critical operation which will largely determine the playing ease of the finished instrument, so be sure it is done accurately. The face of the fingerboard may be flat in cross section or

3-30   Wedging to increase tension on the heel

curved in as much as a 3/32-inch crown. This is entirely a matter of personal taste and preference. Sand the fingerboard out with #600 sandpaper.

Using fret wire, cut twenty frets long enough to leave about 1/8 inch overhang on both sides of the neck. Fill the outer 3/8 inch of the fret slots with Titebond, wipe away the excess, and gently tap the frets in place with a hammer as shown in Figure 3-34 (hold the hammer close to the head for control). The glue prevents the fret ends from springing up if the fingerboard should shrink excessively due to age or low humidity.

When the glue is dry, nip off the overhanging fret wire and file off the ends of the frets as shown in Figure 3-35. Using a long single-cut file with the tang bent up, level the surfaces of the frets as shown in Figure 3-36. A level spot should appear all along the tops of the frets; stop as soon as this is observed. This operation removes any peaks or valleys in the frets caused by hammering in place.

The rounded top surface must now be restored to the frets by filing across the frets with a special fret file which has toothed channels in the

3-31 Gluing on the heel cap

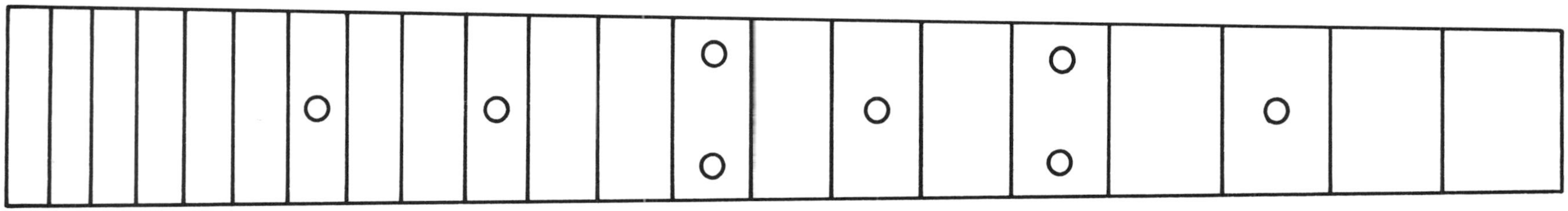

3-32 Inlay pattern

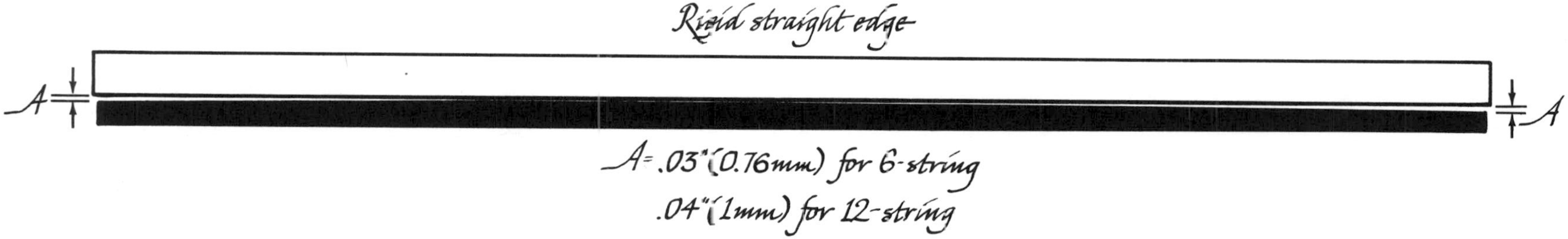

Rigid straight edge

A = .03" (0.76mm) for 6-string
.04" (1mm) for 12-string

3-33 Arching the fingerboard to compensate for string tension

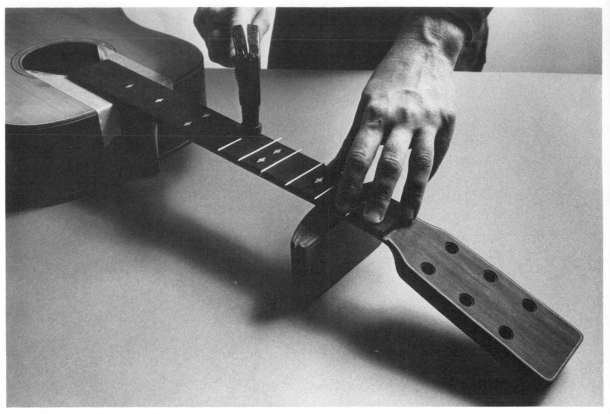

3-34 Tapping frets in place

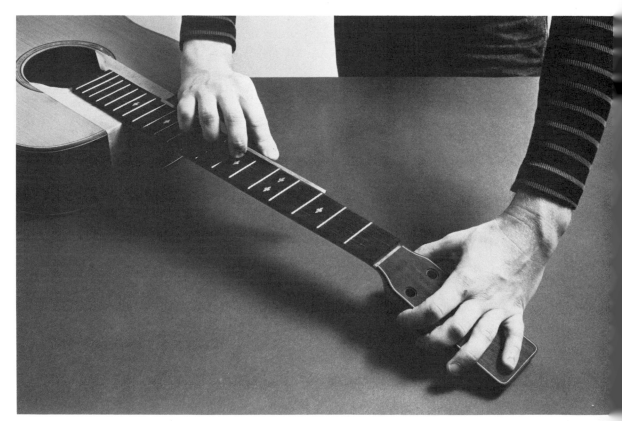

3-35 Filing off fret ends

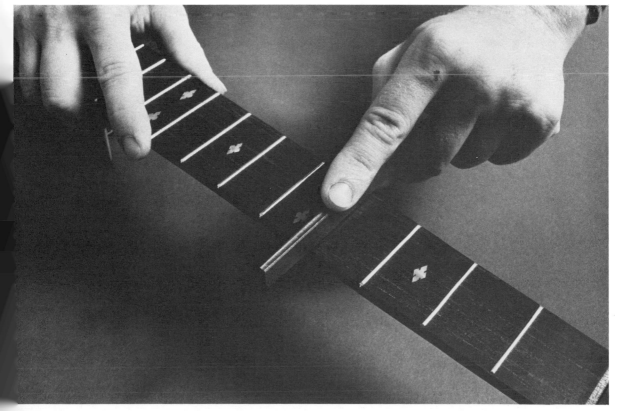

3-36   Levelling frets

3-37   Rounding the tops of the frets

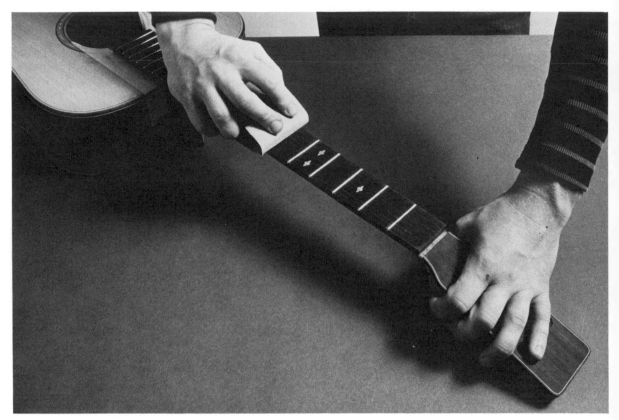

3-38   Polishing the frets

edges. Remove only enough metal to take the flat spot off the tops of the
frets (see Fig. 3-37). Polish the frets by sanding across the fingerboard
using #400 sandpaper followed by #600 sandpaper (Fig. 3-38). Polished
frets are easier on strings and make bending the strings while playing
much more controllable.

MAKING THE BRIDGE

The bridge is made of rosewood or ebony: a block 7" x 1¼" x ⅜" (17.8
cm x 3.2 cm x 9.5 mm) is needed for a six string bridge. A twelve-string
bridge requires a block 7" x 1¹³/₁₆" x ⅜" (17.8 cm x 4.6 cm x 9.5 mm). An important but rather difficult detail is to arch the bottom of the bridge to
conform with the arch of the top. This is easily done on a bench belt
sander by placing a block shaped to the proper curve under the belt. The
shaped block is held in place on the sander with tape which has adhesive
on both sides. The bridge bottom can also be arched by hand with a
scraper.

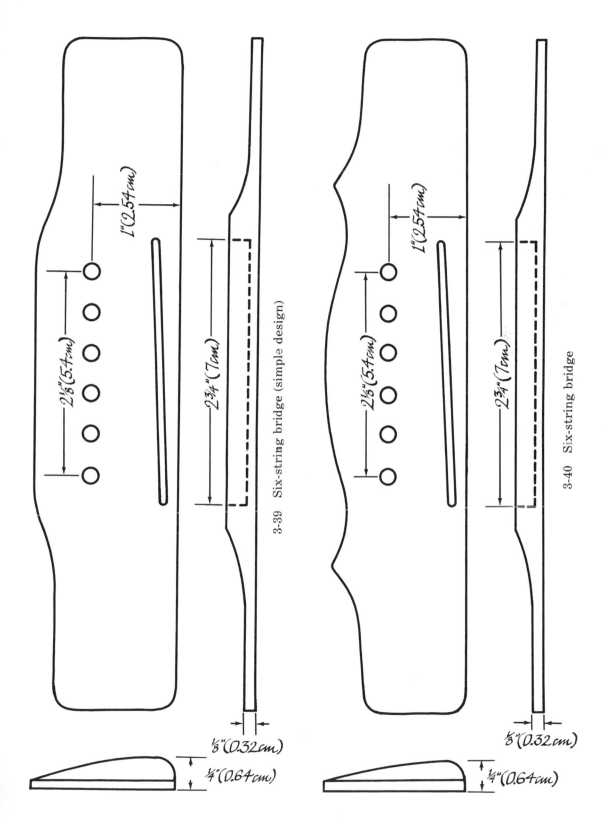

1"(2.54cm)

2⅛"(5.4cm)

2¾"(7cm)

⅛"(0.32cm)

¼"(0.64cm)

3-39 Six-string bridge (simple design)

1"(2.54cm)

2⅛"(5.4cm)

2¾"(7cm)

⅛"(0.32cm)

¼"(0.64cm)

3-40 Six-string bridge

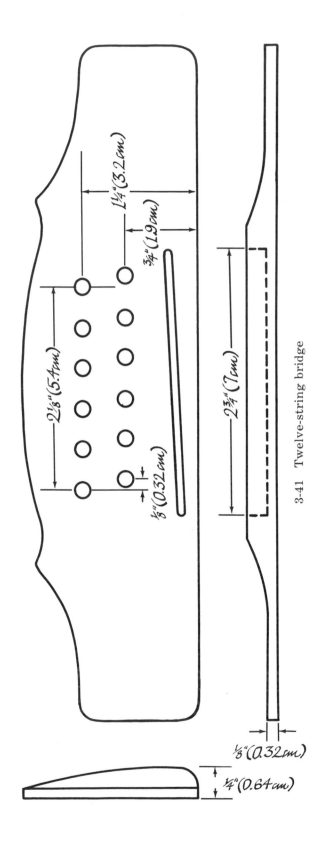

1¼" (3.2 cm)

¾" (1.9 cm)

2⅛" (5.4 cm)

⅛" (0.32 cm)

2¾" (7 cm)

⅛" (0.32 cm)

¼" (0.64 cm)

3-41 Twelve-string bridge

3-42   Routing the slot for the saddle using a drill press

Scribe the outline of the bridge according to Figures 3-39, 3-40, or 3-41. Cut the outline of the bridge with a coping saw or bandsaw and sand the edges smooth. Round off the top and taper the ends to ⅛ inch (3.2 mm) as shown in Figure 3-39. Mark the centers for the bridge pin holes with an awl and drill the holes.

The best way to cut the saddle slot is with an 0.09-inch (2 mm) end mill in a drill press, as shown in Figure 3-42. The slot should be angled to compensate for the pitch change caused by pressing the strings down to the frets when playing. The bass strings are under more tension and require a longer scale length than the treble strings. A special jig is needed to hold the bridge while cutting the slot (see Fig. 3-43). This operation can also be done with a Dremel Moto-Tool on a router base if the bridge and angling jig is clamped to a bench. Figure 3-44 shows the steps in shaping the bridge.

A blind-end slot is stronger than an open-ended slot, and easier to work with when adjusting the action height. Commercially made bridges are available with open-end slots.

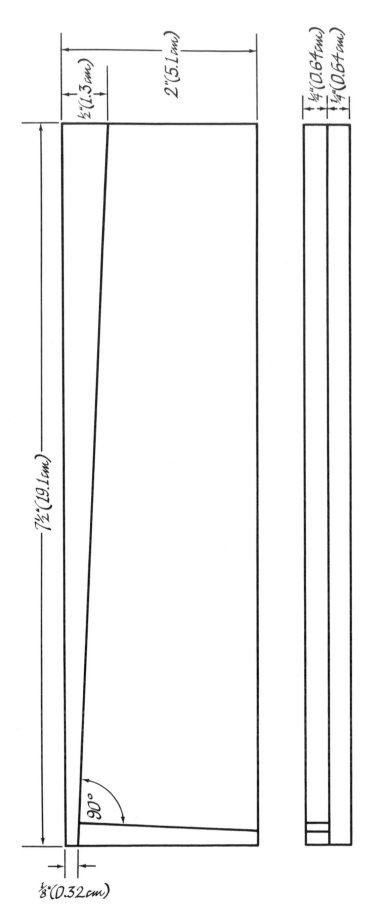

½"(1.3 cm)

2"(5.1 cm)

¼"(0.64 cm)

¼"(0.64 cm)

7½"(19.1 cm)

90°

⅛"(0.32 cm)

3-43   Jig for angling the saddle slot

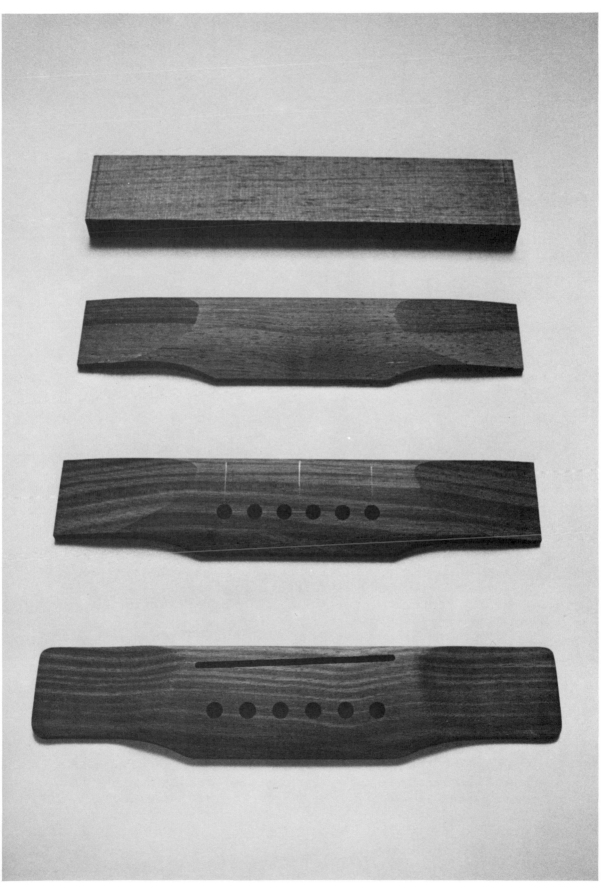

3-44 Stages in shaping the bridge

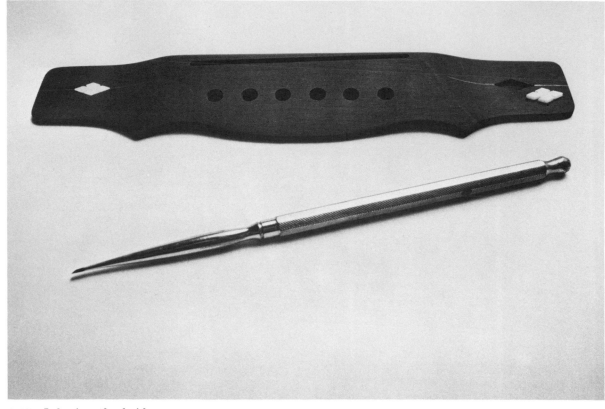

3-45   Inlaying the bridge

If you wish, the bridge may be inlaid with mother-of-pearl dots, or some other type of decoration. Scribe around the inlay and cut a recess for it, using a rotary cutter and/or a small dental chisel such as the one in Figure 3-45. Set the inlays in place with epoxy dyed black with tinting color (lampblack).

To locate the bridge on the top, position the bridge so that the center of the slot is exactly $13^{27}/_{32}$ inches (35.2 cm) from the center of the twelfth fret. Use a drafting triangle to keep the leading edge of the bridge perpendicular to the centerline of the top (Fig. 3-46). Scribe a light line into the top to mark the leading edge of the bridge (Fig. 3-47), and lay a strip of tape precisely along this line so that the bridge may be moved for lateral positioning without changing the scale length. Using a piece of kite string or white thread, center the bridge relative to the fingerboard by holding a piece of thread taut with one end at the edge of the nut end of the fingerboard and the other end centered over the outer peg hole in the bridge (Figure 3-48). Check both sides, and when the bridge is centered,

3-46   Finding bridge position

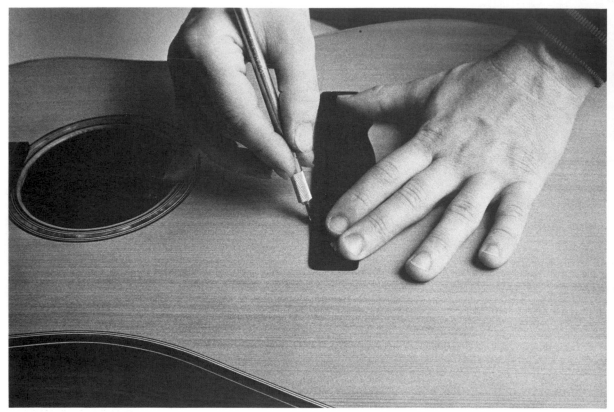

3-47   Scribing bridge position

pin it in position by drilling two holes through the bridge slot and the top, and insert one-inch #18 brads through the holes to act as locating pins during gluing (Fig. 3-49).

Before gluing the bridge to the body, the surface of the guitar must be finished.

3-48   Checking lateral alignment of the bridge

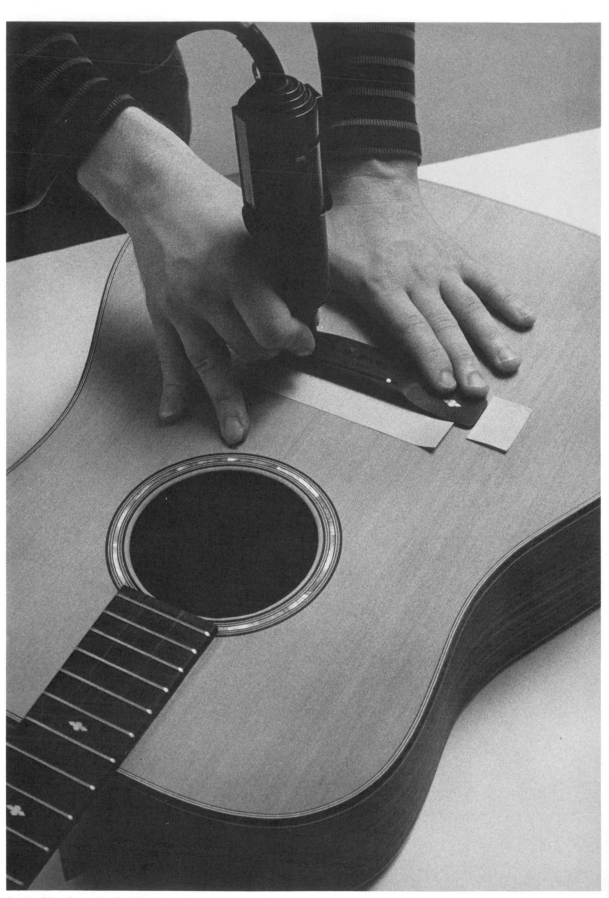

3-49   Pinning the bridge in place with brads

4 Finishing & Adjusting

FINISHING

The first step in finishing the guitar is preparing the surface. Any dents in the top should be steamed out and any chips should be filled with stick shellac (see Chapter 5).

Beginning with #120 paper, sand the entire guitar, using progressively #150 grit, #220, #400, and finally #600. The final finish can be no better than the surface on which it is applied. If you stop short of #600 sanding, there will be scratches visible under the finish.

Before applying sealer, mask off the fingerboard and the area under the bridge. A mask for the bridge area is easily made by laying a strip of 2-inch masking tape on a sheet of formica or glass and scribing around the bridge with a sharp knife. The tape can then be peeled up and placed over the corresponding lightly scribed outline on the guitar top.

Next, seal the entire guitar with clear shellac. Shellac has a short shelf life, so it is best to make a fresh batch by dissolving shellac flakes in alcohol and filtering out the impurities. If this is impractical, prepared shellac is available in dated containers. This "stopping out" coat helps prevent light colored purfling from being stained by the filler.

The pores in rosewood or mahogany must now be filled. Using a dark brown or black filler (such as Sherwin-Williams® paste wood filler dyed with tinting colors), go over the neck, back, and sides, using a fairly stiff brush to work the filler into the pores. Wipe off the excess, working first across the grain, then parallel to the grain to remove any smudges.

When the filler is completely dry, you may begin applying the finish. Varnish can be applied using a fine natural bristle brush; it produces the most durable finish. It has the disadvantage of drying slowly and picking up dust in the process unless kept in an absolutely dust-free place. Varnish must be sanded between coats, using a sanding block where possible to keep the surface fair.

Lacquer is fast drying and easier to apply if you have spray equipment. Spray dry, thin coats of sealer to fill the pores, sanding with #400 paper between coats to keep the overall finish thickness to a minimum. When

4-1　Rubbing out the lacquer with a lamb's-wool buffer

the pores are sealed, spray lacquer until the surface is smooth and fair, sanding between coats with a sanding block where possible.

The number of coats required will vary greatly according to materials, individual technique, and individual pieces of wood. No hard and fast rule is possible, but a good guideline is to apply finish until all the pores and irregularities are filled, then add one or two more coats to allow for final sanding and rubbing.

When the finish is sufficiently hard (about 5 days for lacquer), sand all over with #600 sandpaper used wet with soap as a lubricant. Be very careful not to go through the finish at the edges.

Rub out the finish with a soft cloth and rubbing compound such as DuPont® white auto polishing compound. A lamb's-wool buffer is helpful in bringing up a high gloss (Fig. 4-1).

After the top is rubbed out, cut around the edges of the bridge mask with a razor blade and lift off carefully. Coat the locating brads in the bridge with soap, and glue on the bridge as shown in Figure 4-2. Use Titebond and secure with at least three clamps. Use blocks of scrap to raise the clamps out of the way so excess glue can be wiped away.

4-2 Gluing on the bridge

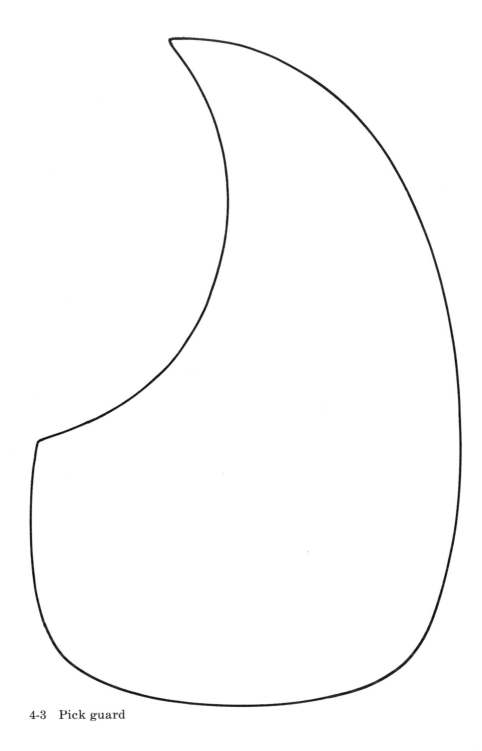

4-3   Pick guard

Using the pattern in Figure 4-3, cut the pick guard out of 0.02 inch acetate and bevel the edges with a scraper (or razor blade used as a scraper) and smooth with #600 sandpaper. Attach the pick guard to the top with Double Avery S-277® self-adhesive plastic (available at stationery or art supply stores). *Don't glue* the pick guard directly to the top: plastics used for pick guards usually shrink with exposure to heat or light, or just with age. This tends to deform and eventually crack the top, a common occurrence on old guitars.

FITTING THE TUNING MACHINES

Tuners for steel string guitars should always be the through-the-peghead type. There are high-quality slotted-peghead type tuners available for nylon string guitars, but these are not suitable for steel string guitars because the large diameter rollers create too fast a tuning ratio. The slotted-peghead type tuners which are made for steel string guitars are generally of inferior quality. The best tuners are Schaller® or Grover® 12-to-1 ratio enclosed gear variety. Next in preference are nylon-cased enclosed tuners made by Schaller. These have press-fit bushings which are hammered in place.

Before fitting the tuners, the finish must be removed from the holes in the peghead. Bevel the edges of the hole slightly with a countersink to reduce the chance of lifting the finish away from the back of the peghead, then ream out the hole with the same drill used to make the hole. If a recess was cut in the peghead as shown in Figure 3-10, the finish must be carefully cleaned out with a tool such as the dental chisel shown in Figure 3-44.

Install all the tuners and tighten the collars finger tight. Make sure they are aligned, then drill the holes for the screws. Don't overtighten the screws; they are often of poor quality and the head may break off, posing an awkward problem of removing the portion embedded in the wood.

ADJUSTING THE ACTION

Drill out the holes in the bridge to the proper size for the bridge pins (this varies with different types of pins) and bevel the edges of the holes with a countersink. Slots should now be filed in the bridge to allow the strings to come out of the pin holes and over the saddle in a smooth curve, as shown in Figure 4-4. This lessens the force which tends to deform the top and decreases the likelihood of cracks between the pinholes, a common occurrence. Should the bridge crack between the pinholes, it can be repaired with epoxy dyed black or brown with tinting colors to match the wood.

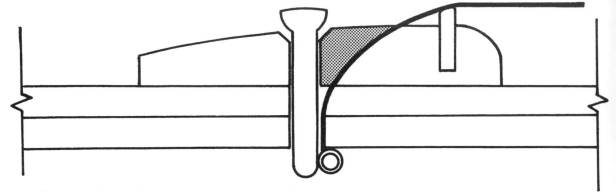

4-4   Cross-section of bridge through the slot filed to provide a curved lead to the
saddle (shaded area)

Cut the ivory or bone saddle to fit the slot in the bridge, and shape the
top as shown in Figure 4-5. Do not use plastic for the nut or saddle;
plastic absorbs enough energy to noticeably reduce volume. Ivory is preferable to bone as the latter tends to turn a dull yellow with age, but ivory
is much more expensive and in short supply. Shape the nut as shown in
Figure 4-6.

The first and sixth strings should be fitted first. They must be just far
enough from the edge of the fingerboard so that they will not slip over
the end of the frets while playing and cause buzzing. This distance is
about 3/32 inch (2.4 mm) from the edge of the fingerboard at the nut (Fig.
4-6). Using a razor saw and needle files, cut the slots for the first and
sixth strings. Fit the strings and tighten them enough to hold the nut in
place. Using dividers, find the positions of the four remaining strings; the
distance from center to center should be equal for all six strings (see Fig.
4-7).

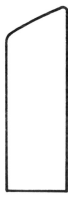

4-5   Cross-section of saddle

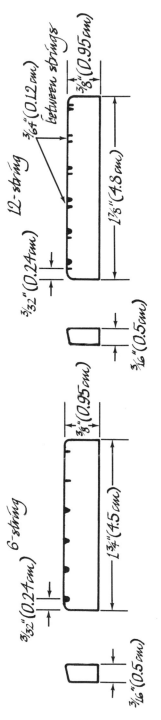

4-6 Six and twelve-string nuts

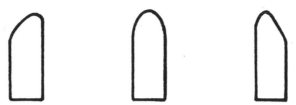

4-8   Changing scale length by altering the shape of the saddle

Cut the bridge slots so that the treble strings are about ¹⁄₃₂ inch (.7 mm) above the first fret and the sixth string is about ³⁄₆₄ inch (1.2 mm) above the first fret.

For a twelve string guitar, the string height at the twelfth fret should be about ³⁄₃₂ inch (2.4 mm) on the treble side and about ¹⁄₈ inch (3 mm) on the bass side. Trim the saddle height until these approximate measurements are reached, then bring the strings up to the correct pitch. Medium or light gauge strings are recommended; avoid heavy gauge strings; they will probably damage the guitar over a long period of time.

Sight along the edge of the fingerboard to check the straightness of the neck. There should be a *very* slight forward bow (concave toward the strings) for optimum playing action, about ¹⁄₆₄ inch (0.4 mm).

If the neck has too little or too much bow it may be possible to correct the problem by changing to a heavier or lighter gauge string. If the bow is uneven, or too extreme to be corrected by a change of string gauge, there is no alternative but to remove the frets and re-arch the fingerboard.

If the neck looks straight enough (and it should), fine adjustment of the action can be done by gradually lowering the saddle height and/or the slots in the nut until the action feels right or buzzes occur. If a string buzzes when played open, it is probably too low at the nut end. Place a thin paper shim under the nut to raise the string to the proper height. If buzzes occur when fretting notes up the fingerboard, place a shim under the saddle to raise the strings. Optimum action varies with the individual's technique and playing style and can only be arrived at through trial and error.

Sometimes one encounters guitars which have mislocated bridges, resulting in the instrument playing too sharp or too flat high on the fingerboard. If the error is slight, the scale length can be corrected by changing the shape of the top of the saddle, as shown in Figure 4-8. Another method for correcting this problem is to fill in the bridge slot by gluing in a piece of wood, then recutting the slot in the appropriate place.

If the error in placement is too great to be corrected by the above means, the bridge will have to be removed, relocated, and glued down after the finish is scraped away from the area underneath. It may be possible to make a slightly larger bridge of the same pattern to cover the unfinished area which would be left by simply moving the bridge.

4-7   Finished mahogany guitar

5　Repairs & Refinishing

CORRECTING WARPED NECKS AND REFRETTING

Warped necks are probably the most common repair problem with steel string guitars. To counteract the pull of string tension, most steel string guitars have an adjustable truss rod. This usually consists of a rod embedded in the neck, anchored at the heel end, with a nut for adjustment under a plate on the peghead (see Chapter 3).

To adjust this type of truss rod, remove the cover on the peghead, and with the strings on and tuned to pitch, very slowly tighten the adjusting nut with a box end or socket wrench (Fig. 5-1). The D and G strings will probably have to be loosened and moved out of the grooves in the nut to allow clearance for the wrench, but leave the other strings under tension. If the neck has an even forward bow and the truss rod is properly installed, tightening the adjusting nut should straighten the neck.

There are several problems, however, that adjustable truss rods will not correct. If the neck is twisted, or if there is a dip or bump where the neck joins the body, tightening the truss rod will not help. Twelve-string guitars with two truss rods are an exception: this arrangement allows for adjusting the treble and bass sides of the neck somewhat independently and can remove a twist.

If the neck cannot be straightened due to the problems described above, or if there is an s-curve in the fingerboard (the reasons for this are described in Chapter 3), the only solution is to remove the frets and sand or plane the fingerboard straight.

Older guitars which have either a solid (nonadjustable) reinforcing rod, or no rod at all, can sometimes be straightened by another method. If the fingerboard was put on with animal glue, the neck can be straightened by clamping it straight and gently heating the fingerboard with a heat lamp. This softens the glue somewhat and allows the neck to straighten. After the neck has cooled, remove the clamps. Let the guitar sit overnight before restringing. This operation may have to be repeated to get the neck completely straight. Unfortunately, this does not counteract the forces which originally warped the neck, so the repair may only be temporary.

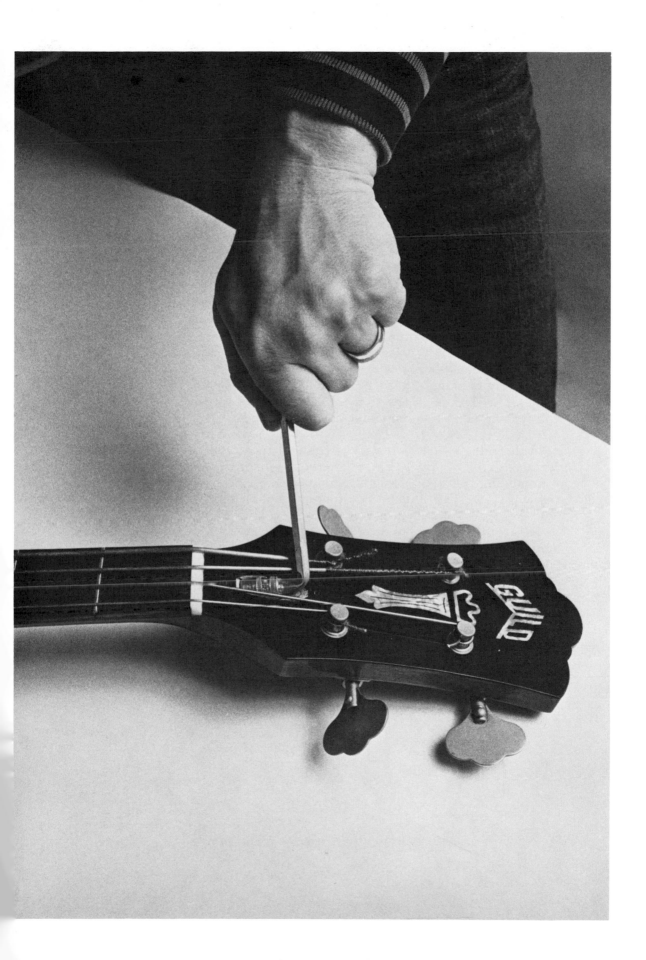

This method does not work if the fingerboard was put on with synthetic glues. Old instruments were usually made with hide glue but more recent instruments are usually made with synthetic glues.

A solid bar can be put in the neck of older guitars which do not have a truss rod by removing the frets and routing a slot through the fingerboard. The bar is glued in with a piece of wood on top which matches the fingerboard. This centerpiece is then slotted for the frets and the job is finished as described in Chapter 3. This method requires a jig for holding the router and should only be attempted by professional repairmen or skilled craftsmen. It is mentioned here because there are some very fine old instruments with badly warped necks which can only be made playable in this way.

A rattle in the neck due to a loose or broken truss rod is usually accompanied by a severely warped neck which must be replaced. However, in the event that the neck is straight but the truss rod still rattles, it may be possible to eliminate the problem by removing the frets, drilling holes through the bottom of the slots into the channel routed for the truss rod, and forcing in glue to immobilize the loose pieces.

If the frets are worn so deeply that the action cannot be adjusted by filing the frets, or if the frets are coming up at the ends, they must be replaced. This is a fairly straightforward job, but there are some pitfalls.

Removing the frets presents some problems. A special tool is needed to remove frets. This can be made from electrician's end nippers or tile cutters by grinding the end flush as in Figure 5-2. This allows the fret to be lifted out of the slot while the ground surface of the tool presses against the fingerboard, preventing the edges of the slot from chipping. Ebony is particularly prone to chipping.

If the frets are difficult to remove, they may have been epoxied or glued in place. To remove glued-in frets, heat the fret gently with a soldering iron (most glues break down between 175° and 200°F). If the fingerboard is bound with plastic, be very careful not to melt the binding.

5-2   Regrinding end cutters for use as a fret removing tool

Once the frets are removed, follow the instructions in Chapter 3. Before installing new frets, clean out the slots and make sure the slots are deep enough to take the new frets; some wood may have been removed when leveling the fingerboard.

REPAIRING CRACKS

The most common type of crack is caused by exposure to low humidity or heat. This causes a split, most often in the top or back. If the crack has not opened so far that you can see through it, it can be repaired by working Titebond into the crack and rubbing the glue over the surface with your finger. Make sure the wood is aligned along the crack, propping one side with a brace as shown in Figure 5-3 if necessary. Clean off excess glue with a damp cloth.

If the crack is more than a few inches long, it should be reinforced by wooden cleats, glued with the grain perpendicular to the crack as shown in Figure 5-4. Cracks in the top, near the soundhole, can have cleats clamped in with a C-clamp. Where a C-clamp cannot be used, a flexible spruce prop can be used as a clamp. This is also a useful technique for

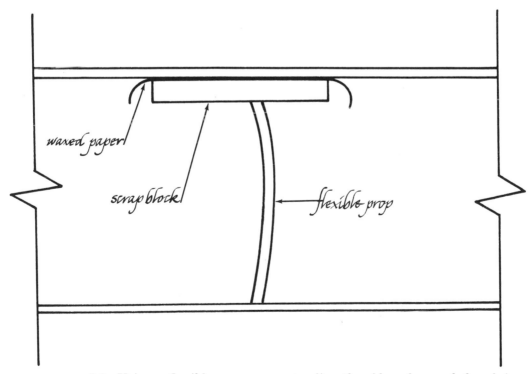

5-3 Using a flexible spruce prop to align the sides of a crack for gluing

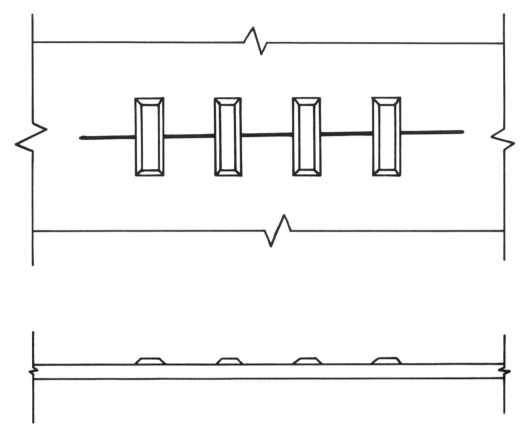

5-4   Reinforcing a repaired crack with cleats

gluing loose braces. Work glue under the brace with a palette knife, then prop it in place as shown in Figure 5-3.

If a crack is separated, it should be filled with a thin strip of matching wood. Open the crack to a uniform width with a saw or the corner of a scraper blade used on edge, like a chisel. Cut a strip of matching wood, tapered slightly in cross section so it will fit tightly (Fig. 5-5). Glue the splint in with Titebond and back it up with cleats as described above.

When repairing any humidity-related crack, it is important to carry out the repair under low-humidity conditions. Otherwise the crack may reappear, either in the same place or nearby, when the next dry spell arrives.

Cracks caused by dropping an instrument or banging it into a sharp corner are often accompanied by deep dents, holes, and lost chips of wood. The cracked portion is repaired as previously described, but a patch may have to be spliced in. The usual shape is elliptical, as shown in Figure 5-6. Avoid patches with points or sharp angles; these concentrate stresses and may provide the beginnings of new cracks. Taper the sides of the

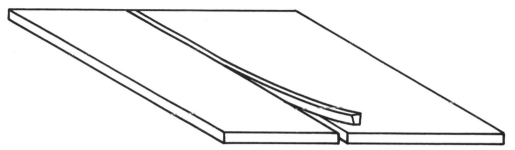

5-5 Repairing an open crack by gluing in a splint of matching wood

patch so it will fit snugly, and scrape it smooth with the surface when the glue is dry.

REFINISHING

There are four important points one should consider before deciding to refinish a guitar. First, it will take a long time for the new finish to dry. During this period, the tone and volume of the guitar will suffer slightly, as the comparatively soft finish will absorb some energy.

Second, refinishing is *more* work than the original finish job, since the old finish must be stripped and any blemishes in the wood filled or steamed out before surface preparation can begin. The bridge should be removed in order to keep the top surface fair and to rub out the finish evenly. This entails some risk of tearing the top wood or cracking the bridge.

Third, a refinish job is seldom as good as the original finish, even if skillfully done. If the instrument is old and of high quality, avoid refinishing it if at all possible since antique instruments are more valuable

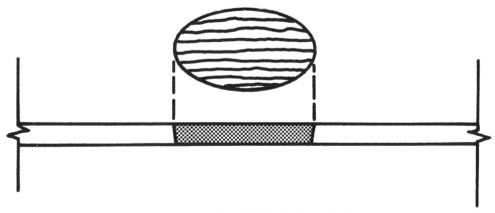

5-6 Elliptical patch for gouged wood or holes

with their original finish. Natural aging produces finish cracks, crazing, and color changes. Unless there is evidence of abuse, these changes can make the instrument more beautiful, just as antique furniture may acquire a rich patina with age.

Finally, refinishing is expensive (a really good refinish job costs $150 or more) because of the amount of work involved. The instrument may be worth less than the cost of refinishing it.

If you still decide that you want to refinish, proceed as follows. Remove the tuning machines, pick guard, and bridge. To remove the bridge, work all around the edge with a stiff, blunt-ended palette knife, using it like a chisel and tapping gently with a hammer. Work the blade slowly under the bridge, and it will eventually pop off. It is normal for some small pieces of the top to come off with the bridge—chisel these away from the bridge and glue them back into the top before proceeding.

Some bridges are fastened to the top with machine screws, particularly on cheap guitars. Look inside with an inspection mirror and check for bolts or protruding screws. This type of bridge can be almost impossible to remove without cracking either the top or the bridge. Try to remove the screws before working on the bridge itself. If this fails, the best policy may be to chisel the bridge off in pieces and replace it with a new one. This is better than risking serious damage to the top.

Remove the old finish with stripper, scraping it away with a putty knife or razor blade when soft. Patches which resist removal may be taken off with fine steel wool soaked in lacquer thinner or mineral spirits (use rubber gloves to protect your hands). When the finish is removed completely, clean the surface thoroughly with lacquer thinner or mineral spirits. Steam out any dents, fill any nicks with stick shellac, and proceed as directed in the chapter on finishing.

To use stick shellac, melt some of the stick onto a palette knife over an alcohol lamp or a candle, and press the shellac into the blemish which is to be filled. It will harden as soon as it cools and can be sanded down immediately.

To steam out dents, wet the wood and heat the area with an ordinary iron, using a layer of damp cloth to protect the wood from scorching. Another method is to attach a rubber hose to the spout of a tea kettle of boiling water. A jet of steam can be directed wherever needed. These methods are very effective for raising dents in soft wood if the grain is not torn.

Glossary

Action: A general term for the degree of ease with which an instrument can be played. It is determined primarily by how straight the neck is and how close the strings are to the frets.

Bout: The portions of the sides that curve outward. The top bouts are the upper parts of the sides between the neck joint and the waist. The bottom bouts extend from the waist to the bottom joint of the sides.

Bracing: Strips of wood which are glued inside the body of the guitar to provide strength and to improve volume and tone quality.

Bridge: A wooden block glued to the top which supports the *saddle* and provides an anchor point for the ends of the strings.

Bridge pins: Small pegs which hold the ends of the strings in place in the *bridge*.

Checks: Small cracks in the surface of a piece of wood.

Cleat: A small piece of wood glued across a crack for reinforcement. The grain of the cleat always runs across the grain of the cracked piece, never parallel to it.

Edge binding: Protective and decorative strips of wood or plastic which are fitted around the edges of the guitar body. They serve as protection against accidental damage and seal the end grain of the wood.

End pin: A peg attached to the sides at the bottom joint, used for attaching a shoulder strap.

Fingerboard: A sheet of hard wood (usually ebony or rosewood) glued on the playing surface of the neck to hold the *frets* and to provide a hard surface to resist wear from strings and fingernails.

Fret: A t-shaped piece of wire with a studded tang, hammered into a slot in the *fingerboard* at a nodal point of the scale of the instrument.

Heel: The extension of the neck perpendicular to the fingerboard where the neck joins the body. It provides rigidity and a large gluing surface for attaching the neck to the body.

Heel cap: A plate of hard wood glued over the end of the *heel* opposite the *fingerboard*.

Jig: A device which holds parts in their proper spatial relationship during assembly.

Lining: A strip of wood fitted around the inside edge of the body of the guitar to provide a gluing surface.

Neck: The "handle" of the instrument, which supports the tension of the strings and provides a comfortable grip for the left hand while playing.

Nut: A piece of ivory of bone fitted at the end of the *fingerboard* next to the *peghead.* It defines one end of the *scale length* and has grooves cut in the top surface which keep the strings properly spaced.

Peghead: The flat area at the end of the *neck* opposite the body of the guitar. It holds the *tuning machines* and provides a point of attachment for the strings.

Pick guard: A thin plate, formerly made of tortoise shell but now made of plastic, which protects the top from damage by the pick or fingernail.

Purfling: A decorative strip inlaid just inside the *edge binding.*

Rosette: The decorative ring inlaid around the *soundhole.*

Saddle: A strip of ivory or bone which fits into a slot in the *bridge.* It provides a hard bearing surface for the strings and defines one end of the *scale length.*

Scale length: The length of the vibrating portion of the string. It is defined by the *nut* at one end and the *saddle* at the other.

Soundhole: The hole in the top of the guitar.

Tuning machines: The pegs to which the strings are attached at the peghead. They are provided with a reduction gear to give greater sensitivity when tuning.

Waist: The portion of the sides that curves inward.

Sources of Supply

Erika Banjos
14731 Lull
Van Nuys, CA 91406

Mother-of-Pearl and Abalone

Albert Constantine and Son, Inc.
2050 Eastchester Road
Bronx, NY 10461

Wood and Tools

Bill Lewis Music Ltd.
3607 W. Broadway
Vancouver 8, B.C.

Wood and Tools

The Wampeter Works
Box 7527
Van Nuys, CA 91406

Wood and Hardware

Marina Music
1892 Union Street
San Francisco, CA 94123

Wood and Hardware

Sherry-Brener Ltd.
3145 W. 63rd Street
Chicago, IL 60629

Wood and Hardware

Vitali Import Company
5944 Atlantic Blvd.
Maywood, CA 90270

Wood, Tools, Hardware

H. L. Wild Co.
510 E. 11th Street
New York, NY 10009

Wood and Hardware

Bibliography

Backus, John. *The Acoustical Foundations of Music*. New York: W.W. Norton, 1969.

Helmholtz, Herman. *The Sensations of Tone*. New York: Dover, 1954.

Hill, W. Henry. *Antonio Stradivari*. New York: Dover, 1963.

Hutchins, Carleen M. and Francis L. Fielding. "Acoustical Measurement of Violins." *Physics Today*, July 1968.

Kasha, M. *Complete Guitar Acoustics*. Tallahassee: Cypress Cove Press, 1973.

_____. "Adventures in the Physics of String Instruments." *Britannica Yearbook Science and the Future*, 1974.

Morse, Philip M. *Vibration and Sound*. New York: McGraw-Hill, 1948.

Perlmeter, Alan. "Redesigning the Guitar." *Science News*, 98 (1970), 180–181.

Winckel, Fritz. *Music, Sound, and Sensation: A Modern Exposition*. New York: Dover, 1967.

Wood Handbook. U.S. Department of Agriculture, U.S. Government Printing Office, Washington, D.C., 20402.

Index

David Young lives and works in Los Angeles. He holds a B.A. in Psychology from UCLA, where he also studied music. In addition to academic studies, two years were spent studying classic guitar performance under Frederick Noad.

A self-taught luthier, he has made over one hundred guitars, a number of which are played by prominent recording artists.

The design philosophy in constructing these instruments is to incorporate classic guitar mechanical integrity, ornamental taste, and playing sensitivity into the steel string guitar.

The author's other activities include playing Go and the study of Aikido.